S0-ADQ-268

"I believe the doctor of the future
will be a teacher as well as a
physician. His real job will be to teach
people how to be healthy. Doctors will
be even busier than they are now
because it is a lot harder to keep
people well than it is just to get them
over a sickness."
—*Dr. D. C. Jarvis*

These books are
not only informative—
they are interesting
reading. — At least
I think so!

Love

Fawcett Crest Books
by Dr. D. C. Jarvis:

ARTHRITIS AND FOLK MEDICINE

FOLK MEDICINE

Arthritis and Folk Medicine

by D. C. Jarvis, M.D.

FAWCETT CREST • NEW YORK

Copyright © 1960 by D. C. Jarvis

Published by Fawcett Crest Books, a unit of CBS Publications, the Educational and Professional Publishing Division of CBS, Inc. by arrangement with Holt, Rinehart and Winston, Inc.

All rights reserved under International and Pan-American Copyright Conventions. Published in the United States by Ballantine Books, a division of Random House, Inc., New York, and simultaneously in Canada by Random House of Canada Limited, Toronto.

All rights reserved, including the right to reproduce this book or portions thereof in any form.

ISBN 0-449-20509-6

Printed in the United States of America

First Fawcett Crest Edition: June 1962

40   39   38   37   36   35

Contents

This book is dedicated to
my daughter, Sylvia Jarvis Smith, and my grandson,
Jarvis Fred Smith,
to convey to them through the written word
the folk medicine of Vermont
which one generation of native Vermonters, living
close to the soil, hands on by word of mouth to
succeeding generations.

Foreword

AFTER THE PUBLICATION of my book, *Folk Medicine,* I began to get a small flood of letters. They came from every state and from several foreign countries. As I read them I realized that the people who wrote fell into three groups. There were those who thanked me for transferring Vermont folk medicine to the printed page and making it available to others. A second group reported successful experiences with some procedure the book presented, while those in the third group indicated that they could not find in the pages of the book information about treatment for a particular illness.

This third group wanted to know if Vermont folk medicine could help them. Many of these people asked for more details on what Vermont folk medicine said about treating arthritis, and as time went on the number of such inquiries seemed to increase every day. In trying to answer them myself, I discovered that a letter had its limitations and I just could not write in detail all I wished to tell them.

After quite a few attempts to answer these letters fully I decided to put down in another book what Vermont folk medicine has learned about arthritis during the two hundred years of its existence. This knowledge has been passed on by word of mouth from one generation of native Vermonters to the succeeding generation. By passing it on again in these pages to those who suffer from arthritis I hope to convey what Vermont folk medicine would wish me to convey, and I hope sincerely that the knowledge will make life a little easier for all those having arthritis who read it.

D. C. JARVIS

~~~~~~

"I believe the doctor of the future
will be a teacher as well as a
physician. His real job will be to
teach people how to be healthy.
Doctors will be even busier than
they are now because it is a lot
harder to keep people well than it
is just to get them over a sickness."

Dr. D. C. Jarvis

~~~~~~

Chapter One

Arthritis

ARTHRITIS is only a new name for what early Vermonters called rheumatism. Because it is not contagious and seldom kills, doctors do not always give it the interest, attention, and time that they should. It is usually a disease of long duration, too, and so a doctor often finds it hard to keep up his interest in the treatment. For that matter, he is at a loss as to just how he should proceed with treatment, since the cause of arthritis is not fully known. As a result of his repeated failures to relieve the symptoms a medical man is likely to get the impression that arthritis is incurable and he will therefore lose interest in it.

The patient, however, endures all the sustained agony of any other chronic disease. Arthritis does not kill quickly and dramatically, like heart disease, nor does it develop with the slow and certain inevitability of cancer. Arthritic patients often live to a great age, and indeed they seldom die of their disease. Yet they have one common symptom: excruciating pain. When we consider that this pain affects more people than that from any other chronic disease it seems strange that more progress has not been made in understanding the cause of an ailment so widespread and so painful, and in finding a cure for it.

Most of us think of arthritis as a disease of later life, but although elderly people often have it there are a good many others under forty-five who are afflicted. In either case, it is only reasonable to believe that there must be certain definite reasons for the presence of the disease.

There are fundamental laws of body chemistry and physiology that nature requires us to observe. We may be ignorant of these laws because most of us no longer live close to the soil, but that doesn't excuse us from the penalty of failing to observe nature's rules. Instincts brought across the human bridge from our parents guide and direct us during our childhood in observing the natural laws relating to our body's good health. Once we are adults, however, we abandon these childhood instincts, and so we have nothing to guide and direct us in observing nature's laws. As a result, the laws are broken, and sickness and unhappiness begin to appear.

Somehow we find it hard to accept the wise plan nature has provided for us. We rebel against her and try constantly to revise the plan and shape it to our own desires. But it never works. Sooner or later we are punished in the form of sickness, which may sometimes be arthritis. Nature has a way of eliminating humans who break her laws. An individual must adjust to his environment as she intended, or else be sick and perhaps die.

People with arthritis live in a world of pain, helplessness, and confusion. When arthritis strikes, with its agony, swelling, and stiffness, worry and fear must follow. As the pain gets worse the worry grows, and as the stiffness begin to interfere with normal living fright becomes a daily companion. As the unfortunate sufferer struggles to find a way out he encounters only confusion when it comes to treatment. Often he is told there is nothing to be done, that there is no cure for his arthritis.

But is it really so hopeless? Let us turn to Vermont folk medicine and discover what has been learned by the trial and error method of research during the past two hundred years. In doing so we will find out what happens when one ceases to rebel against nature and instead accepts her wisely arranged plan and obeys her laws. Let us relearn these laws by studying honeybees, fowl, and animals, and observe whether arthritis is favorably influenced when the laws are observed.

Chapter Two

Two Schools of Medical Thought

ALL MY MEDICAL LIFE I have practiced in an environment in which there are two different schools of medical thought. One is represented by organized medicine which was taught me in medical school. The other is Vermont folk medicine, which I learned about as I talked with patients who lived on farms.

In medical school I was taught the theory of infection, and I was led to believe that if I applied the theory it would enable me to solve my patients' problems and restore them to health. For a time the orthodox education of a medical man centered almost exclusively on the infectious diseases, and it was perfectly logical that this should be so.

Medicine became scientific with the appearance of the bacteriologist. Therapeutic discoveries were acclaimed if they dealt with specific diseases; of necessity, serums and vaccines played an immense role in the medical as well as the lay mind. Certainly bacteriological medicine proved its worth in solving, one after the other, the problems presented by the infectious diseases.

But today we are confronted with other problems, now that the infections have been largely conquered. In these times we must deal with chronic fatigue, skin diseases, high blood pressure, heart attacks, stomach and intestinal ulcer, and colitis. Hay fever makes hundreds of thousands of people miserable, and so do migraine headaches and arthritis. Cancer remains an unsolved problem. Chronic ailments make up an ever-increasing percentage of medical practice, and the psychoses, too, increase annually. It even appears that we are having trouble these days with the muscles of our body.

I found it fascinating in medical school to study microorganisms, toxines, serums, and vaccines, and to diagnose high-grade, low-grade, and focal infections. But when I went into practice and applied the theory as I had been taught to do, I discovered that I could classify my medical accomplishments under three headings:

1. Patients I could really help
2. Patients I could help only a little
3. Patients for whom I could do nothing

To my considerable disappointment, there were far too many patients in categories two and three.

The reason for my failure, I decided, was that medical treatment centered around the infectious diseases, and it was difficult to understand and treat properly the diseases which now make up the remainder of mankind's ailments. In Vermont folk medicine, however, I recognized a different approach to the solving of medical problems than those I had been taught. As time passed, I decided that a working knowledge of this approach could only add to what I had acquired in medical school, and by so doing would help me give better service to my patients. It might even furnish the key that would open the door to a better understanding of clinical conditions for which I had no efficient treatment, and with better understanding would come better treatment. I was particularly interested in arthritis, because if Vermont folk medicine could help clear up the mystery of that disease it might well prove to be a very useful tool in treating other clinical conditions.

I decided to study Vermont folk medicine seriously, to learn its language and medical reasoning. I cultivated a willingness to prescribe its remedies if they turned out to be as good or better than those I had learned from organized medicine.

To begin my study, I spent five years collecting the remedies used by Vermonters. I found that fruits, berries, the leaves of plants, the bark and roots of trees, balsam, pitch and gum found on trees, honey, and the oils obtained from fowl and animals were used in making these remedies. But after all my collecting I still did not understand the medical reasoning behind their use. Obviously the language of medical school and of Vermont folk medicine were two different tongues.

I asked native Vermonters living close to the soil, particularly those I knew to have inquiring and analytical minds, how I could learn the language of folk medicine. I was told that first I should study honeybees and become familiar with their wisdom. Especially, they said, I should study the feeding, growth, egg-laying ability, and length of life of the queen bee. Then I should study the instincts of wild and domesticated fowl and animals. I should note how instincts guide the deer, and what happens to domesticated animals like the dairy cow when man interferes with her instincts, and how animals are guided and protected by their instincts if they are left to follow them.

My Vermont neighbors advised me to study, as well, the instincts of little children, noting how they liked sour drinks and sour vegetation like rhubarb plant stalks and sorrel. Why, for example, would a little child of four, guided only by instinct, tease for a teaspoonful of apple cider vinegar just as it came from the vinegar bottle and take several teaspoonfuls of it if permitted? I was told to try and understand why small children will buy a sour pickle at the store instead of candy, and even save up money to buy a bottle of pickles, eating all of them and drinking the vinegar left in the bottle.

By the same token, I should examine other natural happenings in the countryside. Why would a dairy cow lick the feed trough for half an hour after cleaning up her ration if apple cider vinegar was poured over the feed when it was placed in the trough? Why would a horse drinking water leave it and start drinking from a pail of apple cider vinegar if it were set down nearby? Why would calves stop chewing the wood of their pen and licking the paint on the barn after apple cider vinegar was added to their drinking water?

I was told, in the fourth place, to study adult individuals living close to the soil whose childhood instincts, carried over into later life, continued to guide and protect them. Conversely, I was to examine the lives of those adults who failed to preserve their early instincts, and observe what happened to them. In doing so I should try to understand why man tends to rebel against nature and to be a deserter from the animal kingdom. Once I understood, I would have to learn how to teach man to accept nature's plan, as the animals and little children do. I should teach him the animal laws and how to be a good animal. When he had learned natural law and accepted it good health would often return to him.

If I made a continuing study of the instincts of honeybees, fowl, animals, and little children, I was told, in time I would learn the medical language of Vermont folk medicine, and when I learned it I would recognize that it was in fact the medical language of nature, designed to guide and protect her children by means of instincts. By understanding nature's language I would be able to ask my medical questions in her tongue and understand her answer, yes or no.

Thus, knowing what I had to do, I set about doing it. I studied honeybees, chickens, hens, minks, cats, two kennels of dogs, a herd of registered goats, two herds of dairy cows, calves, bulls, farm horses, and race horses. I did not come to this research empty-handed. My ancestors had tilled the soil and I had inherited from them a love of the land, of fowl and animals, and an intuitive feeling for nature and her ways. Even with this inheritance it took me ten years to learn the medical language of Vermont folk medicine. Having learned it, I recognized it as the language of the chemistry and physiology of the body. From the beginning it had charted a course that by-passed bacteriological medicine and moved directly toward biochemical and physiological medicine.

Practicing as I did in a rural environment where both organized and folk medicine were represented, it became clear that the former variety was built around the micro-organism and virus—in brief, bacteriological medicine. This is a product of laboratory work carried on by man, and is solidly based on the proposition that the micro-organism or virus is responsible for the production of a great deal of sickness. In this kind of medicine emphasis is placed on the disease itself rather than on the patient who has the disease and the environment in which he lives.

Folk medicine, on the other hand, is a product of nature, carried on in the laboratory of the outdoors—in short, physiological and biochemical medicine. In time, one learns that it is built around the energy-expending mechanism of the body, which consists of the brain, heart, and blood; the thyroid gland in the lower part of the front of the neck; the two adrenal glands, one perched on the top of each kidney; the coeliac ganglion, located in the abdomen; and the sympathetic division of the autonomic nervous system.

These organs and tissues control the expenditure of energy in all animals, including man. They organize the body for aggressive action, both mental and physical. They shift the human motor into high gear. Our modern way of living requires this gear-shifting more than ever in order to do the day's work and meet its needs. But somehow we have lost the knowledge of how to shift gears in the other direction and so we are faced with a group of clinical conditions which might be called energy diseases.

When the human motor is shifted into low gear, these diseases are successfully treated. That is why we must learn again how to do the shifting by taking, during the day, the old drink of Vermont folk medicine made by adding two teaspoonfuls of apple cider vinegar and two teaspoonfuls of honey to a glass of water. This drink, which has survived two centuries of use, satisfies the instinct for acid and sugar that is present in animals and little children. It enables an individual to observe many of nature's laws designed to keep her children free from sickness.

If you study this simple drink from a medical point of view it is surprising how many desirable changes occur when it is taken. Primarily the mixture shifts the chemistry and physiology of the body from an organization for combat to one which is conducive to peace and quiet and the building and storing of body reserves against the day of need.

We can help this process by a wise selections of the foods we eat. We need to shun civilized foods, represented by white flour foods, white sugar, packaged cereals, and processed foods. We need to turn to natural foods that do not come out of a factory, and eat more of fruits, berries, edible leaves and roots, and honey. We need to live more out of the garden, the orchard, and the ocean. The apple cider vinegar cruet needs to be returned to the table, along with the honey receptacle.

Apparently we have lost the knowledge of how to maintain and rebuild the human body so that we can live long, full, and rewarding lives. Somehow we have lost an understanding that the composition of the human body is a mineral one. In spite of vitamins and the good they have accomplished, in the last analysis we must provide a daily intake of minerals to maintain, build, and rebuild our bodies. That can be done easily by taking one kelp tablet at one meal each day, a tablet of the kind that contains only kelp from the ocean. In kelp there are at least sixty minerals or elements, more than twelve vitamins, and twenty-one amino acids—all in balance.

We need to learn again how to produce sleep at night. Better by far than any "lullaby pill" is a cup of honey to which three teaspoonfuls of apple cider vinegar are added. Keep this mixture in the bedroom, and when you prepare for bed take two teaspoonfuls of it. Honey is a sedative. It does not require digestion in the human stomach, because this has been done by the honeybee. Honey is in your blood stream twenty minutes after you have taken it, and usually you will be asleep within an hour after getting into bed. If not, take two more teaspoonfuls of the mixture. Should you wake up after midnight and do not soon fall asleep, take two more teaspoonfuls and you will quickly drift off.

From what I have said in this chapter I am sure it is clear why a combination of organized medicine and Vermont folk medicine in daily practice enables a doctor to give his patients better service than he would if he practiced only one of the two. Organized medicine enables him to be efficient when a bacteriological disease confronts him, and Vermont folk medicine comes to his aid when he must treat such energy diseases as chronic fatigue, high blood pressure, heart attacks, stomach and intestinal ulcer, colitis, and arthritis.

Chapter Three

The Fundamentals of Nature

HAVING INHERITED a love of the soil from my farmer ancestors, I bought a home in Vermont with enough land to make a large flower garden possible. Working in the garden not only gave me pleasure as I studied plant life, but it was also a relaxation from the daily routine of medical practice.

When sickroom and office problems multiplied, it was always refreshing and frequently helpful to turn to nature and study her children: the plants in my garden. Then I could leave behind all the carefully built up theories of medicine and return to the fundamentals of nature that turn seed time into harvest.

Plants are remarkably like patients. The more I studied my garden, the more resemblance I saw. I observed that a single package of seeds might contain abortion, infant mortality, puny adulthood, and robust health. These seeds might all get the same nourishment, light, air, and heat, yet they would develop in different ways. One would germinate and die—an abortion. Others would put out their cotyledons only to wither and die—infant mortality. Still others came to maturity but were always puny; while others lived, fought, withstood harsh treatment, and grew into fine plants.

Similarly, when a doctor has a patient who is a narrow-chested, elderly spinster with a dropped stomach, he is reminded, if he is a gardner, of the puny plant that would not thrive no matter how it was treated.

On the other hand, there are plants that will grow no matter how you treat them. They will all come to maturity and bear flowers at the same time, yet one is only six inches high with a single flower while its sister plant has grown into a bush several feet high with masses of huge blooms.

Plants breathe, feed, and reproduce like human beings. They have their likes and dislikes. Their homes and their young grow up around them. They are born, live, flourish, and die as men do. They give pleasure and profit, or like weeds they only encumber the earth. Young plants are often raised like babies, in an incubator, after which they graduate to the nursery and then go out into the world.

Turning to the patients a doctor sees in the day's routine, it is natural to question whether they are so different from the plants in the garden. Don't they need sunshine, water, and proper food to be healthy? Can't we make the same approach to patients that we make to plants? Won't the fundamentals of nature that apply to plants also apply to patients?

These fundamentals are ages old and have stood the test of time. They tell us that in order to turn seed time into harvest there must be suitable soil, properly prepared; seed of sufficient germinating power or a root with enough strength; a certain arount of moisture, a certain amount of heat, and the soil at rest after preparation and planting.

In the human, body cells represent the soil and its preparation is the daily food intake, the work and the habits of the individual. Harmful germs are the seed. Moisture is the dehydration of the body cells which causes them to lose some of their fluid content, and heat is represented by the presence of fever in the body. The soil at rest results from an altered body chemistry and physiology which no longer enables body cells to accept the food material that comes to them. This is evident in loss of appetite.

A doctor examining his patient tries to find out what has made the body cells become suitable soil for the development of sickness. Is it, he inquires, the daily food intake, the day's work, the patient's habits, or his failure to adapt himself to the environment in which he lives? Germs harmful to the body grow in alkaline soil. Has the normal acid reaction of the urine and the normal acid reaction of the skin changed to alkaline, reflecting a change in the body chemistry and physiology? Is the human motor set in high gear, and does it need to be shifted into low? Are the body cells giving up their moisture? Is fever present? Are the pulse rate and breathing rate too rapid, indicating that the human motor is in high gear?

Approaching these problems from the Vermont folk medicine standpoint means concerning oneself first with the patient and not with the disease. The question then becomes how the body of the patient was made into suitable soil for the development of disease. It is the patient who has the disease, not the disease the patient.

Treatment, often of a simple nature, is prescribed to restore the body processes to their normal ways of functioning. Advice is often given about what the daily food intake should be, or a possible change in work may be indicated, or perhaps the patient needs a better adjustment to his environment. Cold climate fruit juices are prescribed for their acid and mineral content, and herb teas are often recommended, if available, in order to restore body cell function to normal.

This approach of Vermont folk medicine works very well when applied to a patient who has arthritis.

As I studied native Vermonters and their children I observed that the presence in the children of a soil suitable for the development of disease depended to a large extent on the way in which the expectant mother selected her daily food intake during her pregnancy. It seemed to me that an individual had a basic right to inherit from his parents the kind of body tissues that were unsuitable soil for disease production. I thought it grossly unfair to an infant to give him a poor start in life by spoiling an otherwise splendid inheritance through faulty selection of foods during pregnancy.

As I have said, the composition of the body is mineral. Dust we are, says the Bible, and to dust we shall return. If the expectant mother does not give an unborn infant the proper balance of minerals, nature does the best she can with what is given her. We build and rebuild the human body by means of the food we eat, the liquids we drink, and the air we breathe.

This process can be observed in farm animals which are properly fed. By controlling the daily food intake of the mother cow during her pregnancy and pouring two ounces of apple cider vinegar over her ration at each feeding, twice a day, we will get a calf that is on its feet within five minutes after it is born and will be nursing at the mother's udder within a half hour after birth. It will have strong legs and a good deal of hair on its body. The same treatment and the same results can be observed in dogs, goats, and horses which are similarly fed.

When it comes to human pregnancy, however, we forget the nutritional knowledge we have learned by feeding animals. Yet it is demonstrably true that the control of an animal mother's daily food intake has a great deal to do with the body chemistry and physiology of the young animal when it is born.

Thus it is clear that the initial state of human tissues may well determine whether disease will find favorable soil in which to plant itself and flourish. In arthritis, for instance, there is evidence that harmful germs constitute the seed of sufficient germinating power or the root of sufficient strength, to grow in the tissues. At times arthritis begins after an attack of tonsilitis or a severe cold or an infection of the gall bladder. When the cold is cleared up or the gall bladder infection is successfully treated, the pain and swelling in the joints often disappears.

Under certain conditions an infection will also influence an already existing case of arthritis. For example, a person with the disease will feel worse when he develops an infected tooth. In this case the localized infection seems to tax the body defenses, thus aggravating the arthritis. Once the tooth is removed and the infection clears up the aches and pains will diminish but the arthritis is still there, very much alive and active.

There is another support for the theory of infection in the fact that arthritis and infection have much in common. Both produce swelling, redness, tenderness, and heat. Both cause pain at times and a slight fever, with perhaps even an increase in the heartbeat.

Vermont folk medicine believes that the human body gives lodging to millions of bacteria. Certain of these bacteria are harmless and never become a problem. Others are potential evildoers, and only await the proper conditions to cause trouble. Bacteria are constantly present on the mucous membrane of the nose, throat, intestines, and on the skin, not actually growing in the living tissues but in immediate contact with them. Occasionally these normally harmless bacteria overstep their bounds and try to gain their livelihood at the expense of the adjacent living cells. The wall of the intestinal tract is not impermeable to bacteria, and their passage through the wall does take place. Because of its acid reaction, however, the normal stomach is practically free from bacteria.

It is well known that the nature and characteristics of germs are modified or even completely changed with a change of environment. It is also known that the same germs may be harmless or harmful, depending on the environment and the influence that surrounds them. These facts are frequently overlooked or disregarded, yet when properly considered, they place the blame squarely where it belongs, namely, upon the condition of the body which makes up the environment in which the germs grow and multiply. Only when the body is depleted or weakened can germs get a foothold, and only in an environment that is favorable to their growth and development are they able to thrive and become active.

Once this is clearly understood it becomes evident that the condition of the body and not the germs themselves is primarily responsible for the development of a disease. It is equally plain that when the tonsils, the teeth, the intestines, or the gall bladder have become affected, unhealthy body influences also are responsible for the impairment. When these organs are impaired, according to Vermont folk medicine, the need is not for surgery or the administration of remedies that destroy bacteria, but for the application of measures that will rebuild the body and restore normal functioning.

No one questions that specific germs are present in specific diseases. Every organism thrives best in the environment best suited to its needs, or in other words, each environment promotes the growth of its special type of micro-organism. But is it logical to conclude from this that the germs create the environment? Isn't it rather that a diseased or abnormal environment provides a favorable soil for the growth of a particular type of bacteria?

Apparently there are three kinds of tissue soil. First there is the kind in which bacteria find lodging but nothing comes of it. They wither away because they have no roots. Then there is the kind in which bacteria find the soil suitable and grow in it, but the conditions are not favorable because the protecting forces in the body get the better of the struggle. Finally, there is the variety in which the bacteria find the body tissues to be good soil and produce sickness.

Vermont folk medicine believes that apparently there is only one disease resulting from abnormal chemo-physical changes taking place in the body, and this process is the same whether in plants, animals, or man. These abnormal chemo-physical changes produce clinical physiology and body chemistry. The part of the body affected, as well as the tissues and organs showing a change in function, is governed by whether the cells in the part affected succumb to altered physiology and body chemistry.

The cells of the body get the raw materials they need from the food we eat, the liquid we drink, and the air we breathe. The material needed by the cells enters the blood stream from the lungs and digestive tract. In the blood stream this newly acquired material circulates as a biochemical mist which is transferred from the blood through the meshlike walls of the tiny blood vessels called capillaries to a fluid called the lymph, which carries the mist, representing food and oxygen, to the wall of each cell.

When it gets the mist, the cell processes it, utilizes some of it for growth and the performance of cell function, and stores the remainder within itself against the time of need. This process of receiving, processing, and storing takes place in much the same manner as the honeybee changes the nectar from the flowers of the field into honey, as the tree condenses material from the sap into fruit, and as the plant forms seed. All the various bricks used in the construction of body cells are to be found in the blood and lymph of animals and man.

In a healthy body the cells have several functions to perform. They must collect the required quantity of biochemical mist from the lymph which bathes each cell wall, process it, use some of it, and store the rest, as described above. When this labor of the cells is interfered with, disease replaces health. Such interference may result from the lack of a proper quantity or quality of biochemical mist reaching the cells, due to a faulty intake of food, liquid, and air. Then, too, there may be interference with the permeability of the cell walls, or possibly failure to remove cell waste promptly.

Each cell may be subjected to two primary physiological-biochemical changes. These two changes are swelling (hydration) and shrinking (dehydration) of the cell. We can observe this process at work in grapes and raisins. Swelling in grapes produces the full-formed fruit we buy at the store. Shrinking results in the dehydrated grape we call a raisin.

Body cells are like grapes or raisins, depending on whether hydration or dehydration is taking place. As grapes, they are enjoying normal health; as raisins, they have lost their resistance and soon will be the seat of disease. In dehydrated body cells a loosening of the links holding the various constituents together within the cell takes place.

To understand how all this happens it is necessary to know something about the structure and operation of a cell. It is a nucleus surrounded by a substance called cytoplasm which fills it to the wall. Cytoplasm is a colloid system, which is another way of saying that it is an emulsion with particles in a fluid medium. These particles are called colloid particles, and the fluid in which they exist but do not dissolve is known as the disperse medium. Colloid particles are referred to as the dispersed phase, and they are able to take in water and swell—in a word, hydration. Because they both take in and give off water these particles stabilize the cell contents.

Carbon monoxide causes so much dehydration of colloid particles in the cytoplasm that sometimes the particles are driven from the colloid state into a true solution. When that happens to an individual, he will die.

Colloid particles have three functions—attraction, storing, and radiation—and their activity may be divided into pre-colloid and postcolloid. When the three functions are carried on harmoniously within the cell health is the result, but if there is disharmony disease follows.

What is it that loosens the links which make up each particle? A broad range of causes will do it, including microorganisms, viruses, allergens, climate, weather changes, the make-up of our daily food intake, emotional upsets, an unhappy environment, family maladjustments, and prolonged physical or mental work. When any one of these factors loosens the links the result is that energy, water, and various bricks making up the particle are liberated. A portion of the liberated energy is freed in the form of electricity, which undergoes ionization through combining with water and is converted into heat, giving rise to fever. We call this process dehydration, because water is liberated.

Another result of loosening the links is that some of the bricks making up the particles go into solution, and if the dehydration is sufficiently great the particles in the cytoplasm pass from a colloid to a crystalline state. The combinations and complexes which fail to be excreted or to go into solution, may be deposited in the tissues, while any particles left behind in the cytoplasm will agglutinate. These various stages of dehydration cause the cell to change from a grape type to a raisin type.

Vermont folk medicine calls for bringing about the rehydration of such cells, so that they will be changed back to the grape type. If suitable treatment is prescribed, the stages of dehydration of the particles and of the watery medium in which they exist may be reversed. The phases of agglutination disappear as water reënters the cell, and the links which hold the particles together become stronger. Bricks then become available with which to form new particles, and eventually enough of them will be restored in the cytoplasm so that they are again dispersed properly. Hydration causes dispersion, enabling the needed materials to enter the cell and resulting in the restoration of health.

The chemo-physical changes of dehydration constitute a regressive phenomenon, while those associated with hydration and rehydration are progressive. In other words, the more regressive the phenomenon, the greater the dehydration and consequently the greater likelihood of a change taking place in the respiratory system.

The micro-organisms which cause dehydration can be divided into two classes: those present in the lower bowel which cause infection from within; and those which have to be implanted in the body before they are able to produce signs and symptoms, causing infection from without. No sharp dividing line can be drawn between these two groups.

Micro-organisms, viruses, and allergens must have material with which to maintain themselves, and they get it by dehydrating the body cells. The contest between these cells on the one hand and the micro-organisms, viruses, and allergens on the other determines whether the cell hydration process is strong enough to dehydrate these invaders or whether the hydrating ability of any one of the three is strong enough to dehydrate the body cells. Suitable treatment will help the cells to win their battle by making their hydration process dominant, with the result that the micro-organisms and viruses die and the allergens are no longer effective.

The putrefactive and disease producing germs which cause so much trouble in the body find it easy to grow under slightly alkaline conditions, but they have a hard time growing under slightly acid conditions. When the acid is of the right kind, such as apple cider vinegar, it may actually destroy them and clear them out. The very fact that germs are handicapped by acid and stimulated by alkalies should in itself make the treatment measures of Vermont folk medicine seem reasonable.

Some individuals may fear that a harmful acid state may be produced in the body by taking the acid found in fruits, berries, edible leaves and roots, honey, and apple cider vinegar. There is no reason to fear. One of the fundamental characteristics of the human body is its maintenance of a state approaching neutrality. This is accomplished chiefly because of one important property of the blood: its function as a buffer solution, which means that extremely large amounts of acids may be absorbed by the body without producing in any way an acidity of the blood. In fact, the blood is far more resistant to acids than to alkalies. It will tolerate a large amount of acid but little of the alkalies. It is possible for the blood to be hyperalkaline or hypoalkaline in reaction. When it is more alkaline it becomes thicker.

There is a normal weakly acid reaction of milk as it comes from a dairy cow. When it changes to alkaline it will thicken up and be like soup. Then flakes will appear in the milk, and these flakes join together to form little lumps. After that, streptococci germs appear.

A farmer who wants to know whether the normal acid reaction of a cow's milk has changed to an alkaline reaction can find out by adding one tablespoonful of soap powder to a quart of water. Soap powder is very alkaline in reaction, and the addition of a single tablespoonful to a quart of water makes a solution that is heavily alkaline. This solution is poured into a cup until it is about one-third full. Then three or four squirts of milk from one of the cow's teats are milked into the cup, and the cup is swished around until solution and milk are mixed, after which the whole thing is poured into a pail.

If the cow's milk is acid in reaction, as it normally should be, the soap powder and water solution in the cup will be thinned and will pour like water from the cup. But if the milk has changed to an alkaline reaction, when the contents of the cup are poured into the pail the solution will be thicker. It may be stringy as it is poured out or it may curdle in the cup. At times the cup solution may become almost solid, like jello. After the test the cup should be well rinsed out before the next test is made.

From this simple barn procedure it becomes evident that acid thins an alkaline solution, but the addition of such a solution to one that is already alkaline makes it thicker. Is it possible that a dairy cow, with her chemical wisdom, seeks only acid reaction vegetation when she is in pasture because she wishes to thin the fluids in her body? Does she avoid alkaline vegetation because she does not want to thicken her body fluids and make their movement in her body more difficult?

I have taken so much space to describe the manner in which each body cell carries on its vital activity because in treating arthritis Vermont folk medicine tries to work through the cell. Its simple treatment measures are intended to return each cell to a harmonious interworking of attraction, storing, and radiation, and to maintain the grape type of cell while avoiding the raisin variety.

Chapter Four

Observations

AS I CONTINUED MY STUDY of farm animals I occasionally observed the presence of arthritis in some of them. It interested me a great deal, and led me to inquire among aged Vermonters, living close to the soil, how I might learn what Vermont folk medicine thought about the cause and treatment of arthritis.

They told me to study, first, what took place in the teakettle when water was boiled. Then I was to examine what happened when sap from the sugar maple tree was boiled in the sugarhouse to make maple syrup. After that I was to see what occurred when an eggshell was covered with apple cider vinegar.

I began by going to the teakettle, as they had advised. In my part of Vermont the drinking water, whether it comes from spring or river, is rich in calcium and contains a trace of iron and magnesium. That is because of the large deposits of lime, marble, and granite beneath the soil. So great is the amount of calcium in the water that when it is boiled a deposit forms on the inside of the teakettle which becomes so thick in time that it hinders the heat from getting to the water promptly to boil it. Usually the deposit has to be removed every two months so that water will boil quickly enough. Native Vermonters have learned by trial and error that deposited calcium in the teakettle enters into solution again in an acid water.

In order to create acid water it has become the custom

to add one quart of water and one cupful of apple cider vinegar to the teakettle and allow it to boil. During the boiling the deposited calcium enters into solution again and is removed when the water in the teakettle is poured out. If the deposit is excessive more than one boiling of the vinegar-and-water solution may be necessary in order to remove all the deposited calcium.

What happens to water when it is boiled in the teakettle? It becomes alkaline in reaction. In this alkaline reaction water, calcium is no longer held in solution but leaves the water in the teakettle to form a deposit of calcium on the inside of the container. When the water is made acid by adding a cupful of apple cider vinegar the calcium deposit enters into solution again as the acid water in the teakettle is boiled.

From this observation I learned that calcium leaves a deposit when water is alkaline in reaction, and enters into solution when it is acid in reaction. On this phenomenon Vermont folk medicine bases its use of apple cider vinegar taken by mouth and applied locally to joints when arthritis is present in the body.

People who have an oil burner with a hot-water coil learn that the coil becomes filled with deposited calcium in a year's time. When the coil is soaked in apple cider vinegar the deposited calcium enters into solution in this acid medium and the burner becomes usable again.

FURNACE OBSERVATIONS

I turned from my study of the teakettle to the method used by plumbers in freeing the inside of a furnace's water compartment from deposited calcium.

Here was the plight of the teakettle all over again. Water in the furnace would no longer boil quickly because there was a thick coating of calcium on the inside of the water compartment. The plumber tested the water with a paper that told him whether it was acid or alkaline in reaction. He had learned that calcium was precipitated when the reaction of the water was alkaline, but entered into solution when the water was acid in reaction. The deposit could have been prevented by making the water acid in the first place.

If the plumber found the water to be alkaline then he added enough apple cider vinegar to shift the reaction to acid and allowed it to boil. After boiling the water he drew it off and replaced it with fresh water which he made acid by adding apple cider vinegar.

At the end of a week the plumber returned and tested the water to find out whether the reaction was still acid. If he found it alkaline he once more added enough apple cider vinegar to shift it to acid.

This change in the reaction of water when it becomes hot may be demonstrated by holding a strip of nitrazine paper in the water as it comes from the hot faucet, and similarly another strip in the stream from the cold-water tap. Here in Vermont the cold water does not change the color of the nitrazine paper strip, indicating a faintly acid reaction. When the strip is held in hot water, however, its color changes to blue, indicating an alkaline reaction.

THE EGGSHELL OBSERVATION

The first step in making a common liniment which follows the Vermont folk medicine recipe is to dissolve an eggshell in apple cider vinegar. You place the two halves of an eggshell in a small glass jar and add enough apple cider vinegar to cover both of them, after which you put the top on the jar. Bubbles will begin to rise very soon from the eggshell to the top of the fluid, and the outside of the shell will be covered with many blisters of various sizes. Within a day or two the shell will have disappeared, leaving behind a thing membrane. The calcium in the shell has entered into solution in an acid medium furnished by the apple cider vinegar.

THE MAPLE SUGAR TREE SAP OBSERVATION

In spring of the Vermont year sap is gathered from sugar maple trees that have been tapped. In the sugarhouse this sap is boiled until it becomes the consistency of maple syrup. Because of its sugar content the sap is very rich in calcium.

Sugar has an affinity for calcium. While a thousand parts of water will take up one part of calcium, it easily absorbs thirty-five times as much calcium when sugar is added. Thus, when sugar maple tree sap is boiled to make maple syrup, the calcium malate in the sap is precipitated and forms what is called in Vermont "maple sugar sand." In order to remove this precipitation the syrup is run through a felt filter about a half-inch thick. When the sap is boiled it becomes alkaline in reaction, just as water does. In this alkaline medium the calcium in the maple sugar tree sap is no longer held in solution but is precipitated to form the maple sugar sand.

MILK FEVER OBSERVATION IN DAIRY COWS

Milk fever is a common, widespread, serious, and acute disease of dairy cows. It usually occurs soon after calving, and affects only the high producing cows in the majority of cases. It is accompanied by a low blood calcium content thought to be brought about by the sudden onset of milk secretion. The disease often recurs following every calving in cows with a previous history of milk fever, but it rarely occurs at the first calving. Untreated animals are likely to die within a short time.

The symptoms are dramatic and pitiful to see. A cow becomes restless before or after calving, staggers, falls, and becomes unconscious. Her eyes are glassy and she is more or less paralyzed, especially in the hind legs, and is finally unable to swallow.

Fortunately the treatment given by a veterinarian is highly successful. Calcium gluconate is injected into the blood stream as soon as the first symptoms are observed. The injection is sometimes repeated if it is necessary. As a rule, dairy cows that are treated immediately after the first symptoms appear to recover very quickly.

When I began studying a mixed herd of fifty-four dairy cows the owner told me that milk fever was common among them and represented one of his worst problems. He hoped I would be able to help him control it, and added that he thought it was caused by a lack of calcium in the cows' blood.

I told him it was hard to believe this was the origin of the disease because the drinking water was so rich in calcium. More likely the same thing was taking place in the cow's body that occurred in the teakettle, the hot-water coil, and the furnace's water compartment. In blood that was too alkaline, calcium would be precipitated and would not be available for normal use by the body.

As I remarked earlier, instinct leads a dairy cow to select her food so that she maintains a proper acid-alkaline balance in her body. I spent many hours following cows in pasture, armed with a gadget which made it possible to put leaves, blossoms, or grass in at one end of the device and, by turning a crank, get juice at the other end, which I could test with nitrazine paper to learn its reaction.

I discovered, by this kind of experimenting, that the cows in the particular herd I was studying always ate vegetation that was acid in reaction, and refused to eat whatever was alkaline. The observation demonstrated that, by always eating acid reaction vegetation they were trying to lessen the alkalinity of the blood. The cows in the herd worked hard. I learned at the local creamery, where their milk was delivered, that they produced more milk per cow than any other herd whose milk was brought there.

Dairy cows like apples, and so I discussed with the owner the advisability of pouring apple cider vinegar over the ration of each cow at each feeding twice a day, after the food had been placed in the trough. I remembered what happened to the water in the teakettle, and I wondered whether the addition of vinegar to feed would cause the calcium to enter into solution again and make it available when it was needed to solve the milk fever problem—if, indeed, the disease was caused by low blood calcium.

There was a small-sized Jersey cow in the herd whose barn name was "Paralyzed," because every time she gave birth to a calf she developed milk fever, with its associated paralysis. The veterinarian was always able to save her with an injection of calcium gluconate. At her previous pregnancy, however, this cow had become paralyzed twelve hours after giving birth to her calf and did not get on her legs again for four days.

"Paralyzed" began getting apple cider vinegar poured over her ration in two-ounce amounts at each feeding, twice a day, on the first of November. She gave birth to a calf during the following February, and this time she was in labor for only ten minutes, proving that the tissues of her body were elastic and would stretch easily. After the birth she got to her feet and began eating. The milk fever never appeared. I could only conclude that the vinegar had prevented the development of a hyperalkalinity of her blood, with the result that the calcium was no longer precipitated but was held in solution so that it was available for use when needed.

During the winter the owner of the herd I had studied reported that his neighbors were having trouble with milk fever but his herd was free from it. He believed it was due to the use of apple cider vinegar, which he was now pouring over the feed of every cow.

I told one of my farmer friends about this experience. He came to my office later to say that one of his cows had developed symptoms of milk fever, and he had given her extra doses of vinegar by mouth out of a bottle. The symptoms had disappeared.

My friend naturally began to use the vinegar with the feed for all his cows, as prescribed. After he had been doing this for a year and a half we agreed to try the experiment of stopping the vinegar treatment for two months and noting what happened. That, we believed, would tell us whether the great improvement in the herd's performance was due to the treatment or to other factors. We also wished to find out whether it was a wise use of money to buy apple cider vinegar in barrels to be poured over the cows' rations.

Before the two months had passed, milk fever returned to my friend's herd. Along with this came other bovine troubles: a drop in milk production and an increase in the bacterial count of the milk. My friend was convinced, as I was. He bought a year's supply of apple cider vinegar and resumed the treatment. Milk fever disappeared.

OBSERVATIONS MADE ON BODY GROWTH

I interested myself next in learning whether growth of the body framework could be influenced by taking apple cider vinegar in order to make calcium available. Two bulls were selected for the experiment, one a Holstein and the other a Jersey. Holsteins develop a larger body than Jerseys, so the vinegar was given to the Jersey bull calf. One tablespoonful of apple cider vinegar was added to three quarts of water twice a day for the calf to drink. Later, as it increased in size, one tablespoonful of apple cider vinegar was also poured over the ration twice a day.

With the bull's growth larger amounts of vinegar were added to his diet. His Holstein companion was not given the treatment at all. When both were fifteen months old the body of the Jersey bull was seven inches longer, even though the Holstein would have been longer in the normal course of events.

Next I selected a Jersey heifer calf, and on the day after its birth I started it on the vinegar, one tablespoonful in three quarts of water twice a day. Later, as the calf grew older and larger, I followed the pattern by pouring another tablespoonful of vinegar over her ration twice a day, making a total of four tablespoonfuls daily.

This calf grew so fast in length, height, and size of head that she soon had the body outline and characteristics of a cow. Instead of being a short-bodied, pot-bellied calf, she had a long body. When she was fifteen months old she was so large that it was possible to breed her and start a pregnancy. Jersey heifers are usually not large enough to breed until they are eighteen months old.

About this time, in February, the mother of a 4-H Club boy who had a Jersey heifer calf as his project happened to be in my office. I asked her how the boy was getting along, and she told me he was pretty worried because the calf had lost its appetite. I told her to ask the boy to add a tablespoonful of apple cider vinegar to three quarts of water twice a day and have the calf drink it.

Two months later she was in my office again and I asked about the calf's progress. Its appetite had returned, she said, and another son who owned a Jersey heifer calf had also begun to feed vinegar to his animal. Before the treatment both these calves had been addicted to eating sawdust and their bedding; they had also chewed wood and lapped the paint on the side of the barn. Now they had stopped doing all these things.

The 4-H Club supervisor came to check up on the project calves, and he was so impressed by their condition that he inquired what the boys had done to raise such fine looking calves. One of the boys told about the vinegar treatment, and the supervisor said he doubted that a calf would take vinegar. To prove it, one of the boys offered a teaspoonful to each calf. Both took it and lapped the spoon. Everyone who came to the barn later commented on the excellent appearance of these animals.

The second and younger calf had been born in September and the vinegar treatment started the following February. Although it had been very small the vinegar made this calf grow so rapidly that by June 30th she was larger than any other calf her age that had not had the benefit of the treatment. She had developed a long body and looked like a miniature cow. When she was only nine months old this calf had an udder as large as a heifer would have a month before producing her first calf.

The 4-H supervisor told the boy with the project calf that his animal was the best one seen so far that season, and at the county fair in September it took first prize. The cattle judge told its proud owner that it was the nicest Jersey calf he had seen that year.

A further confirmation of all this came to me recently in a letter from one of my medical friends who has a herd of Guernsey cows. "You will be interested to learn," he wrote, "that three months ago we had two Guernsey calves born two weeks apart. The older calf was distinctly stronger. The younger calf was a very delicate calf when born. This younger and more delicate calf has been given apple cider vinegar in the drinking water and has now caught up in growth so that she is nearly the full size of the other calf and looks unusually well. This is an interesting observation and is passed on to you for what it is worth."

I applied the lesson of the calves to children who had stopped growing or were growing slowly, and observed that taking a tablespoonful of apple cider vinegar in a glass of water at each meal generally resulted in an increased rate of growth. I recorded an increase in height of as much as two inches in six months' time.

Going back to my observation of cattle, I decided to find out whether the addition of two ounces of vinegar to the ration of each cow in the mixed herd of fifty-four would influence the calf during the period of pregnancy so that it would get a good start.

As cows that had been given the vinegar during pregnancy began to give birth to calves several differences were readily apparent. These cows had an easy labor, lasting about ten minutes. The calf was strong, vigorous, and of good size. Its legs were strong and it had a lot of hair on its body. It got up on its legs quickly within five minutes after it was born, and was nursing at the mother cow's udder before it was a half-hour old. It was, besides, very alert and intelligent. No one had to teach it to drink from a pail.

As these calves grew and later gave birth to their own first calves it was noted that they manifested the milk and butter fat production record they were supposed to inherit from their parents. No longer was there an interruption of the hereditary characteristics that were rightfully theirs. During their lactation period it was observed that each heifer had a vigorous digestion and a good nervous system.

Among humans it has been noted by Vermont folk medicine that pregnant mothers who have taken a teaspoonful of apple cider vinegar in a glass of water at each meal have also had an easy labor. The babies had plenty of hair on their heads when they were born, and could raise their heads off the pillow before they were a week old. They digested food, eliminated it, and slept as a normal infant should.

As these children grew, it was noted that they had a good digestive system and a good nervous system. They all seemed to be very bright mentally and very alert. They not only had strong bodies but strong minds.

OBSERVATIONS MADE WHEN A BULL CALF WAS DEHORNED

A bull calf is usually dehorned when it is ten months old. If it is done before then the horns are apt to grow and form stubs. But when a Jersey bull calf ten months old that had been given apple cider vinegar every day was dehorned, it was discovered that his horns were solid, there was no central opening in them. Apparently the vinegar had improved the use of calcium in his body with the result that his horns were solid.

OBSERVATIONS OF TARTAR DEPOSIT ON THE TEETH

Whenever I found patients who showed a tartar deposit on the tongue side of the lower front teeth they were directed to add a teaspoonful of apple cider vinegar to a glass of water at each meal and to sip this during the meal, so that by the time they were finished with the food the vinegar would be consumed too. They were asked to report to me after the next visit to their dentists.

When the reports came in they were all alike. Those who had taken the vinegar and water for several months reported the dentist found no tartar on their teeth. If they had taken the treatment for shorter periods of time the amount of tartar was less than usual.

One of my patients, a retired lawyer, had an accumulation of tartar that was solid across the inside of his lower front teeth before he took the vinegar-and-water treatment. This deposit disappeared within ten weeks when apple cider vinegar in a glass of water was taken at each meal.

But more surprising than reports on the absence of tartar were the statements from some patients that, for the first time in their lives, the six months checkup by their dentists showed no dental decay at all. One seventy-one-year-old patient who had taken the treatment was given a clean bill of health by her dentist for the first time in her life. She had taken a teaspoonful of apple cider vinegar in a glass of water at each meal for six months.

Other patients reported the number of cavities to be filled was less than usual. I could understand now why the Italians living in Barre, Vermont, had such beautiful teeth. They used wine vinegar and drank sour wine, acidifying their daily food intake as nature intended should be done. All the various fowl and animals I have studied showed improvement in body health when apple cider vinegar was added either to their drinking water or food.

Still other patients reported that their fingernails no longer were subject to bending, breaking, or tearing. Using scissors, nail clippers, and nail files showed that the nails were now thicker than they had been. If white spots had been present on the nails they now disappeared, and the nails also grew much faster than formerly. Continued observation of the nails showed that it took about two or three months of the vinegar treatment to stop their bending, breaking, and tearing.

Patients taking the vinegar also began reporting that their hair had stopped combing out more than normal, and many new hairs were growing in, resulting eventually in an increased amount of hair. It took about two or three months to stop the hair combing out more than normal and to bring about the growth of new hair.

What does Vermont folk medicine conclude from all the

observations I have related in this chapter? It observes that calcium is held in solution by an acid like apple cider vinegar and by a sugar like the sap from the sugar maple tree. Translating these observations into everyday use it prescribes adding two teaspoonfuls of honey and two teaspoonfuls of apple cider vinegar to a glass of water to be taken with each meal, in order to influence favorably the use of calcium in the body. This combination of apple cider vinegar and honey in a glass of water at each meal has been the staple of Vermont folk medicine for more years than any of us now living can remember.

Chapter Five

What Becomes of Calcium Precipitated in the Body

I DISCOVERED that an old butcher who ran a slaughterhouse was in the habit of letting a cow which was to be slaughtered for beef drink a gallon of apple cider vinegar on the day before she was to be killed. Why? Because, he said, the meat would be very tender and have a delicious taste. Without the vinegar, the meat would be tough and tasteless. That kind of information interested me.

As I continued to study Vermont folk medicine I learned that some native Vermonters spent considerable time in teaching the younger generation how to give their bodies thoughtful care. They were taught how to keep themselves always in good physical condition so that the body tissues would continue to be tender and the elasticity of muscles and other tissues would be maintained. That would enable them to age slowly and come to the later years of life with good eyesight, good hearing, good mental and physical vigor, and no immediate appearance of senility.

To teach their children proper care of the body Vermonters had to look no further for examples than the daily life of the farm. The hen and dairy cow, for example, were prime illustrations of how the tissues of the body could be made tender and the tissue fluid be maintained in a proper state.

An aged hen would be killed and served as food on the family table. After it was served and eaten, the attention of the young Vermonter would be called to the fact that the meat was very tough and had a poor taste. That, he would be reminded, could happen in essence to a human as he grew old.

Later, a second aged hen would be brought to the family table, but this one would have been given special treatment before it was killed. In the morning, in the presence of the young Vermonter, the hen's mouth had been opened and a teaspoonful of apple cider vinegar poured down her throat. In the latter part of the day, before roosting time, another teaspoonful of vinegar was administered. That treatment was repeated every day for three days, and on the fourth day the hen was killed and brought to the table.

Now the attention of the young Vermonter was called to the unusual tenderness of this old hen's meat, and its delicious taste. It was a graphic demonstration of how apple cider vinegar, taken by mouth, tenderizes the body tissues.

When meat is needed for the family table during the colder months of the year in Vermont, a cow is slaughtered. As is common with native Vermont beef, the meat is tough and has a poor taste, a fact duly pointed out to the farm boy. But at the next meal he goes to the kitchen where meat from this cow has been soaked in apple cider vinegar before cooking, or if it is boiled, the vinegar is added to the water in which the meat is to be boiled. Brought to the table, it proves to be more tender and have a better taste.

Later, when another cow is selected for slaughtering, she is given the treatment which calls for two ounces of vinegar poured over her ration at each feeding twice a day. This practice is continued for a week before the cow is slaughtered, and the meat turns out to be unusually tender with an excellent taste.

The owner of the herd of dairy cows I studied told me that one of them, ten years old, was to be slaughtered for beef when her present lactation period was finished. During that period she had not been giving enough milk to make her a profitable cow, and so she was to be slaughtered and her place in the herd given to another animal.

There is a rule in Vermont that one year of a dairy cow's life equals seven years of human life. Applying that rule, the cow in question was as old as a seventy-year-old human. I asked the owner how long he expected it would be before the lactation period ended, and he estimated three months. Each one of the cows in the herd was then getting the vinegar treatment in their daily rations. I asked if he would let me know when the slaughtering occurred and he said he would.

When the cow was slaughtered, her carcass was delivered to the local grocery store meat department, and the butcher said the meat would be used to make hamburg. Next day I got some of that hamburg and asked my daughter to try it. She reported it was particularly tender and had a most delicious taste. The butcher also took some of the meat home and made a similar report. I asked my secretary to try it out on her family, without telling her that it had come from a ten-year-old cow. The four adults at her table all commented on the hamburg's tenderness and taste.

The farmer, as was his custom, kept for his own family the heart and liver of the cow. I was especially interested in the heart, wondering whether the vinegar treatment would have made it as tender as the other meat. I asked the farmer to report on the matter, and he told me that this ten-year-old heart was as tender as that of a two-week-old calf's.

As a result of being able to make the meat of slaughtered cows tender by means of the vinegar treatment my farmer friend got five cents more a pound over the market price for the carcasses of the cows and bulls he delivered. The butcher made a list of the customers who liked tender steak, and whenever he got one of the "vinegar carcasses" he notified them he had a special treat.

From observations such as these the native Vermonter assumes that calcium is precipitated in the body in an alkaline medium, as it is in the teakettle, and may be made to enter into solution again when apple cider vinegar is given to fowl, dairy cows, and humans.

When calcium is precipitated in the body tissues of a hen or a cow the animals become tough and tasteless. But when apple cider vinegar is given to them, the precipitated calcium enters into solution again, making the body tissues tender and enhancing the taste. It may be added that when body tissues hold all the precipitated calcium they can, it next appears in the bursae and joints of the body to produce bursitis and arthritis.

The lesson taught a young Vermonter is that by taking

apple cider vinegar each day in a glass of water at each
meal, or used on food, the body tissues will be made very
tender and the tissue juices will be normal. As a result he
will always be in good physical condition and will age very
slowly.

The lesson taught me was that the instinct for acid I had
observed in fowl, animals, and little children was given by
nature for a very definite purpose. The intake of acid by
fowl and animals and the liking of sour drinks by children
was to keep calcium in solution in the body and not allow
it to precipitate and produce toughness of body tissues and
to alter body tissue juices. When this natural instinct was
denied, I assumed, it meant the beginning of degeneration
of tissue in body organs, with a lessening of their ability to
carry on their vital function.

To check further the ability of a dairy cow to do better
work when her body tissues were freed from precipitated
calcium I selected a registered Jersey cow fourteen years old,
the equivalent of a ninety-eight-year-old human. Two ounces
of vinegar were poured over her ration twice a day. She
then produced forty pounds of milk a day on twice-a-day
milking for the first time in her life. She made 441 pounds
of butterfat in 322 days, the best record she had made in all
the years she had been a member of the herd.

To confirm this experiment I took a second registered
Jersey cow, also fourteen years old, and gave her the same
treatment. She produced forty-one pounds of milk a day on
twice-a-day milking, and again it was the first time for her.
She made 414 pounds of butterfat in 299 days. A ten-year-
old registered Jersey made 488 pounds of butterfat in 323
days with the help of apple cider vinegar.

From this study it seems reasonable to conclude that when
a herd of dairy cows in winter quarters in the barn cannot
have the normal contact with nature which it does in the
warmer months, then apple cider vinegar poured over the
ration in two-ounce amounts at each feeding twice a day is
an excellent substitute for acid reaction vegetation which
the herd seeks when it is on pasture.

When calcium is precipitated in the human body we note
the appearance of muscle cramps. These are very painful,
commonly occurring in the legs during the night. They may
also appear in the stomach, intestines, and heart. The taking
of two teaspoonfuls of apple cider vinegar and two of honey
in a glass of water with each meal allows the precipitated

calcium to enter into solution, and the muscle cramps disappear.

Evidence that calcium enters into solution when apple cider vinegar is taken can be shown by changes in the bony structure of a cow's body. A cow that gets the vinegar treatment of her food will be found to have much larger bones than normal when she is slaughtered for food. It is compact bone, with little porous bone present. It is possible to add from fifty to a hundred pounds to a cow's weight by increasing the size of the bony framework through the vinegar treatment. The increase in weight of the bony structure depends on the length of time she has been given the vinegar.

The meat of such a cow will be dark red in color, and the tallow very white. When the bones are sawed through the bone marrow will be a much darker red in color than the bone marrow of cows serving as controls. The butcher I have mentioned before was certain that the vinegar treated beef he got did not come from pure Jerseys because their bones were so large. But it was these large bones which stood as mute evidence that they were a storehouse for calcium.

Chapter Six

A High Protein Intake

SEVERAL YEARS AGO, while I was a house guest of the late Professor George W. Cavanaugh, professor of chemistry at Cornell University, I remarked to him during a conversation, "I'm familiar with the medical end of streptococcus sore throat, but I'd like to learn something about the dairy side of it. Would you tell me something about the problem?" He said he would be glad to, and then came a statement wholly unexpected.

"In a high producing cow," Professor Cavanaugh said, "you have streptococci in the milk any time you care to feed the cow a high protein, low carbohydrate ration."

"Will you please repeat that statement?" I asked, astonished.

He did so, and noting my surprise he went on to tell me that the experimental work on the problem of high protein-low carbohydrate feeding had been done by Dr. Fr. Wiedman, at the Research Institute of the Agricultural Control Station in Regensburg, Bavaria.

Professor Cavanaugh informed me that dairymen depend on high protein feeds to speed up milk and butterfat production. Increased daily rations raise the protein intake of high producing cows beyond the safety line. High protein feeding generally means the underfeeding of carbohydrate. In most cases a high protein feeding schedule results in a carbohydrate deficient ration.

The importance of other elements in dairy rations has been so emphasized that the carbohydrates have often been thrust into the background. However, the trouble that follows underfeeding of carbohydrates can be definitely identified. One effect, in particular, is the loss by cows of one or more quarters of the udder, which is often ascribed by owners to incomplete milking or to cows catching cold or simply to "poor milkers." The real cause is a high protein-low carbohydrate ration.

Professor Cavanaugh gave me an explanation. Briefly, he said, high protein-low carbohydrate feeding does not result in a visible change in the milk at first, but by means of a chemical test the changes can be observed in the composition of the milk as it begins to vary from normal. The normal amounts of milk sugar and fat decrease more and more as the carbohydrate deficiency persists. In an extended feeding schedule based on high protein this would be the case.

The decrease of the fat and milk sugar may continue to the point where both disappear from the milk. The only visible signs of approaching trouble may be the thin appearance of the milk, and perhaps in a fat test the content will be lower than usual.

When carbohydrates are low in a ration there soon develops a separation of the ingredients in the milk. The milk itself may become bloody, and the fat content entirely disappear. The protein particles in such milk separate and settle to the bottom. While this is occurring gradually chemical tests show an increase in the salt content until the acid property of the milk, which normally destroys bacteria, is entirely changed to an alkaline condition.

Here the micro-organisms begin to play their part, first as destroyers of tissue within the teat, and next as carriers or spreaders of the disease called mastitis. Apparently the first requirements for successful bacterial growth are heat and alkalinity. In the laboratory micro-organisms are artificially propagated. In the cow's udder, where the changes described are going on, heat is always present. This alkaline condition favors bacterial growth, and we have ideal conditions for micro-organisms to develop.

I asked Professor Cavanaugh where the prize-winning herd for the United States was located. He told me that the best herd of fifty cows or over was at Cedar Grove, New Jersey, and I asked if it would be possible for me to visit this farm. He said it was, and with his help I went to Cedar Grove, with the objective of asking the herdsman in charge just one question.

On the morning of my arrival I visited two neighboring herds, and in the afternoon we looked over the prize herd, while I studied the butterfat and milk production records of individual cows.

Then I got down to the key question I had come to ask. "Do you have mastitis in your herd?" I asked.

If he answered yes, I knew it would mean the presence of streptococci in the milk.

"I can have mastitis in my herd or not have it, just as I wish," the herdsman answered. "I can feed the herd one way and have it, or another way and not have it."

"Well, if it isn't a secret, how do you feed them so they don't have it—and I presume that's the way you do feed them."

He laughed and said it was no secret. He added fish meal and seaweed to the herd's ration, and depended on protein for butterfat and milk production. He had learned that by adding seaweed, in the form of kelp, and fish meal to the herd's ration he could keep the protein part of the ration four points higher than he would be able to do otherwise, and at the same time his herd remained free from mastitis. This ability to maintain a high protein content in the herd's ration and thus to keep all the cows producing milk had enabled him to win national honors for butterfat and milk production in herds of fifty cows or more.

As I studied dairy cows I learned that when a high protein-low carbohydrate ration is fed to a high producing cow she is very likely to develop swelling in one or more quarters of her udder as time passes. The milk will first change from its normal weakly acid reaction to an alkaline reaction. When this reaction appears, the watery character of the milk changes, becoming thicker like soup. Then, if the milk is poured into a cup which has a fine mesh screen across its top flakes will be deposited on the screen, which later join together to form little lumps until finally streptococci germs appear in the milk, making it unsafe for human use.

In the days when bloodletting was a form of medical treatment in Vermont and elsewhere it was learned that protein food—milk, eggs, cheese, meat, fish, and poultry—thickened the blood and apple cider vinegar thinned the blood. As a result of this observation a nutritional custom was developed that required an acid to be served with protein food in order to lessen its thickening influence.

In accordance with this custom apple cider vinegar was, and is, poured over baked beans. Cranberry sauce, which contains four different acids, is served with fowl. Apple sauce, which contains malic acid, is served with ham and pork. Mint sauce, whose basis is vinegar, is served with lamb. A slice of lemon is served with fish and other seafood. Mushrooms, which contain citric acid, are served with steak.

Protein food not only thickens the blood but also produces a cloudy urine in the majority if individuals. If urine is passed into a glass this cloudiness will be seen when the urine has cooled to room temperature and is held up to the light. If the cloudiness is due to a high protein intake it will disappear when one or two teaspoonfuls of apple cider vinegar are added. An individual with cloudy urine can dissipate it by reducing his daily intake of high protein food—milk, eggs, cheese, meat, fish, and fowl. By experimenting he can determine the amount and kind of protein it is safe for him to take each day.

Vermont folk medicine assumes that urine is modified blood. If the urine is cloudy, the blood also is cloudy. As everyone knows who remembers his schoolbook physiology, the blood in the body makes a complete circuit every twenty-three seconds, but if protein intake has thickened it and made it cloudy it passes through the capillaries more slowly. Higher blood pressure is the result.

Blood pressure is taken to find out if it is higher than it should be, and if it is one must determine whether it has risen because too much protein food has been taken during the day. Two teaspoonfuls of apple cider vinegar are added to a glass of water which the patient drinks. At the end of a half hour the blood pressure is taken again. If protein intake is the cause of the rise the systolic pressure—that is, the pressure when the heart contracts and pushes out blood into the arteries—will drop from twenty to forty points, and the diastolic pressure will also be lower.

If possible, another reading is taken an hour after drinking the vinegar-and-water solution, to learn if a further drop in pressure has taken place. Taking the solution, as you can see, simply observes the old custom that requires an acid to be taken with protein food, and it answers the question as to whether delayed observance will manifest itself in a lower blood pressure.

To keep calcium in solution, as well as to prevent blood thickening and a rise in blood pressure, add two teaspoonfuls of apple cider vinegar and two of honey to a glass and mix it well by stirring with a spoon. Then the glass is filled with water and stirred again. Take the mixture during a meal, as you would a cup of coffee. Just as the prize-winning cows were given kelp and fish meal, a human can take one kelp tablet at breakfast and another at the evening meal to handle better the protein food which the body takes in.

Fish and other seafood represent protein best suited to the human body. Remember seven gallons of ocean water and the composition of the human body are equal.

An individual may discover that a certain protein may be more difficult for his body to handle, and will be more likely to produce a cloudy urine. By the process of elimination he can learn what protein foods his body accepts best, and by observing the old Vermont custom of an acid taken with protein food he will be much less likely to develop high blood pressure.

Chapter Seven

Your Instinct for Acid

IF APPLE CIDER VINEGAR produces the results observed in humans and animals, is there present an instinct for acid which we may have lost?

I answered this question for myself by studying honey-bees, fowl, and animals, and as I have said earlier I learned from them that it was possible to rediscover natural instincts and to comprehend nature's plan by which she intended to keep all her children in continued good health, free from sickness, and able to live the allotted span of life.

Anyone who takes the trouble to learn this plan is inevitably brought to an understanding of the importance of body chemistry and physiology, and the need of safeguarding the body in order to keep it adjusted constantly to both the external and internal environments.

We must—and I emphasize it again—learn not to rebel against nature, not to desert from the animal kingdom. We must accept nature's plan and stop trying to rearrange it according to our own desires. We must be concerned with the food we eat, the liquid we drink, and the air we breathe, because all three influence our body chemistry and physiology, either favorably or unfavorably. We build and rebuild our body with these elements, and so we should give them the consideration they deserve.

Armed with this kind of understanding, we would shun fruits and vegetables sprayed with insecticides and become believers in organic farming. We would avoid refined foods, like white flour and white sugar, and seek natural foods. We would go to health stores as a source of natural foods. Part of our understanding would be that the daily food intake provided by nature is a natural high carbohydrate-low animal protein intake, and so we would become more vegetarians and less meat eaters. Our source of protein would be cheese, eggs, fish, and other seafood.

We would recognize that the dairy cow, like other animals, is endowed with some uncanny capacity for selecting what she eats. When she chooses a plant family like the clover and takes it completely while another plant family is disregarded, she is demonstrating her capacity as a capable chemist. She is reporting her recognition of the high nutritional values in one plant species in contrast to the low nutrition of the other. We have been slow to realize that the cow is a chemist analyzing the soil, with refinements in the analysis that science cannot duplicate.

While I was following my herd of dairy cows in pasture I was impressed by the way they went about selecting their food. They seemed to have a knowledge of chemistry that man has lost, if he ever had it. I recall one field that had a part of it fertilized with acid phosphate as a trial fertilizer. Every year, for seven years, the herd would go directly to that part of the field and graze there before returning to the rest of the pasture. Dairy cows, like honeybees, must have a chemical intuition that we fail to have. They seem to select their daily food with the object of balancing it from a chemical point of view.

I observed four other things during my study of dairy cows in pasture:

1. Cows selected certain spots of ground on which to graze and carefully avoided other spots.
2. They ate where growth was most recent, as represented by buds, flowers, small leaves, and short grass.
3. They did not eat grass growing where manure had been dropped by a cow, although the grass growing on that spot was greener and taller than the surrounding grass. It was strange to see cows avoiding this tall grass, yet eating shorter the short grass around it.
4. Dairy cows did not eat the seeds of plants. It became increasingly evident that they had a chemical sense which enabled them to determine what they should eat.

With the gadget I have spoken about which enabled me to test juice from flowers, leaves, and grass, I tested the reaction of the grass growing on the spots of ground which the herd selected to graze. It was always acid in reaction. Then I tested the reaction of the grass growing on the spots of ground cows avoided. It was always alkaline in reaction.

The testing went on with the same results: the leaves and flowers they ate reacted as acid; grass growing on the manure spots was alkaline.

I went to the field where hay was growing. Horse, cow, and hen manure had been spread on the ground as a fertilizer, and when I tested the reaction of the hay I found it was alkaline. Beside this field was another belonging to an adjoining farm, but it was not being used because the farm's owner had died. When I tested the grass there I found it was acid. No manure had been spread on this land.

From these tests it was apparent that the dairy cows in the herd I was studying were obliged to eat in winter quarters an alkaline reaction hay which they refused to eat when they were able to select their own food in pasture. Again this confirmed my conclusion that cows have an instinct

which leads them to select acid reaction vegetation and refuse the alkaline reaction kind.

I turned next to a study of young cattle in pasture. Would
they seek the same kind of vegetation? I asked the herds-
woman in charge of a herd of forty-five registered Jersey
dairy cows I studied if she would be willing to fertilize part
of one pasture with cow manure, and as soon as there was
vegetation ready to be grazed, turn the young cattle into the
field in order to determine whether they would be guided by
instinct and avoid the manured portion.

She agreed, and in time sixteen head of young cattle were
turned into a pasture about one-fourth of which had been
fertilized with cow manure the previous fall. The manure
had been under the barn for a year, and the part of the pasture where it had been spread had produced grass much
greener and taller than in the rest of the field. It was easy to
see the dividing line between the two parts.

Of the sixteen young cattle, which ranged in age from six
months to a year, only two grazed in the manure fertilized
part of the pasture. These two were about six months old.
But even as I stood watching them, they left the manured
part and began grazing in the other portion. Apparently
even in young cattle an instinct was operating which led
them to avoid the alkaline reaction grass. Nor was this instinct lost when a young cow became old enough to become
a milk producing member of the herd. It was carried over
into the cow's adult life, to guide and protect her.

I wondered how long the instinct persisted in a cow, and
at the same farm I had an opportunity to learn the answer
to my question. In the herd was one cow twenty years old.
For sentimental reasons she was to have a place in the barn
as long as she lived. This aged cow, called Bobby, was given
the run of the farm. I spent some time following her with
my juice producing gadget to learn her eating habits. She
was very fond of acid vegetation, especially elm tree leaves;
she ate them in preference to all other leaves.

It was customary to tie Bobby loosely in the barn so that
it would be easier for her to lie down and get up. One day
she broke loose. Going to the feed car she tried to get into
the apple cider vinegar pail kept there. We all heard the
rattling of the pail and came to investigate. Curious to see
what she would do, we placed the pail on the floor of the
feeding car and she proceeded to drink from it until, satisfied, she turned away. This seemed fairly convincing proof

that the instinct which leads young cattle and adult dairy cows to seek acid is present in an aged dairy cow right up to the end of her life.

After noting how the chemical wisdom of dairy cows led them to seek out acid I wondered how it would be with bulls, which were often kept in the barn. I placed a pint of apple cider vinegar before a bull and he took the whole pint. Then I put a quart of the same vinegar before another bull and he took the whole quart. Obviously bulls were given the same chemical instinct to seek and accept an acid.

I wondered if apple cider vinegar added to the drinking water would appeal to chickens and hens, so I added a fourth of a cup of vinegar to each gallon of water in the henyard. They accepted it at once, and any white diarrhea that had been present in them stopped at once. The hens and chickens drank twenty-five to fifty per cent less water when apple cider vinegar was added to their liquid intake. I noticed that the addition made them feather out more quickly and grow rapidly.

Cats and dogs also accepted one-half to one teaspoonful of apple cider vinegar added to their ration once each day. A small cat got a half teaspoonful, while a large one took a whole teaspoonful. Similarly, a teaspoonful was enough for a small dog, but a large one could take a tablespoonful.

Farm horses, too, so it proved, had the same instinct for acid. One day a pail containing apple cider vinegar was set down near a farm horse that was drinking water at the time. He sniffed at the pail, then turned from the water to the pail and began drinking vinegar.

We tried the addition of two ounces of vinegar poured over the rations of two farm horses at each feeding. The result was most interesting. When the vinegar was used, the horses would leave half their ration; when it was not used, they would eat all of their feed. Their appetites remained good; they simply appeared to be satisfied with less food. But after the vinegar had been added for a time, their heads came up and they developed a fine glossy coat. They had more wind and strength, too. No longer were they a stumbling, pokey team, but alert and ready to pull a load.

From animals I turned to a study of little children under five years of age, knowing in advance that there was a self-protective instinct in young children which impelled them to seek foods needed at the moment by their bodies. My study showed that it was the same instinct that led young cattle, mature cows, and aged cows to seek acid reaction vegetation and avoid the alkaline variety.

As I studied the instincts of these small children I learned that they liked sour drinks, particularly two teaspoonfuls of apple cider vinegar and two teaspoonfuls of honey in a glass of water.

I discussed the children's acid preferences with their mothers and found that more mothers had to hide the vinegar bottle than the sugar bowl when the children were left alone at home. Children will pour apple cider vinegar into a dish and then eat crackers or bread that has been dipped in the vinegar.

In studying native adult Vermonters I learned that the instinct for acid was often carried over from childhood into adult life. This was plain enough from the barrel of apple cider and the other barrel of apple cider vinegar to be found in most farm cellers. The vinegar cruet was always on the family table so that it could be used on food or added to a glass of water, and a glass of apple cider was often taken one or more times daily. When company came, a pitcher of apple cider, apples, and popcorn were the refreshments.

From Vermont farmers I found out about the value of apple cider vinegar in relieving physical fatigue. They told me that when they were tired, they used apple cider vinegar on their food at the two best meals of the day for three or four days. At the end of that time they would usually feel all right again. They also told me that when they found they were tired while working on the farm they went into the house and added some vinegar to a glass of water and drank it. In about an hour the tired feeling either disappeared or was greatly diminished.

A farmer who made apple cider vinegar to sell told me it was not unusual to sell a farm family sixty gallons of it a year. The members of a family using that amount were never sick. They were tough, and ate the vinegar on everything, including green peas and custard pie.

I was curious to know whether there had been any change in the use of apple cider vinegar in the cities and villages of Vermont during the passing years. I found a retired businessman who had been in the wholesale grocery business all his life and asked him if the demand for vinegar had changed during the years he had been in business.

He told me that in the fall of 1903 he would order five carloads of vinegar in barrels to supply his customers. Forty years later, when he retired, vinegar in barrels was no longer in demand. The largest size he bought for his customers was in glass gallon containers, for which there was a limited demand.

Having observed in fowl, animals, and little children the presence of an instinct that leads them to seek an acid, it seems only reasonable that we adults should be better food chemists than we are. If we carried the instincts of our childhood over into adult life, as primitive peoples do, we would include more acid in what we eat and drink. As a result of our failure to do so our body chemistry is often upset. Lack of acid allows body fluids to thicken while the intake of acid thins these fluids, allowing them to move with greater ease in the body.

Translating this instinct for acid into everyday use we turn to apple cider vinegar and honey, both of which are acid in reaction. Both make body tissues tender and create normal tissue juices. Body fluids are prevented from becoming thick and cloudy.

Calcium, as we have seen, enters into solution in an acid medium. Two teaspoonfuls of vinegar and two of honey are first added to a glass and stirred with a spoon until they are well mixed. Then the glass is filled with water and stirred again. The contents of the glass are taken during each meal, sipped like water or coffee. This combination may be taken at a morning coffee break or at tea in the afternoon. But if no time is available during the day, it may be taken on rising in the morning and again at bedtime.

Sickness is not always caused primarily by harmful germs and viruses. It may be the result of an altered chemistry that creates in the body suitable soil for harmful germ and virus growth. An animal that has a normal body chemistry and physiology has very little to fear from harmful germs and viruses. Dairy cows in winter quarters are more likely to be sick than when they are on pasture and able to get acid vegetation. We have observed how the health of a herd can be improved by adding vinegar to the feed during the winter months. There is a marked reduction in the colds, influenza, pneumonia, and digestive tract troubles which otherwise might affect them.

These, in sum, are the lessons I have learned from my observations of animals and children in Vermont.

Chapter Eight

The Dairy Cow as an Experimental Animal

DURING MY STUDY of Vermont folk medicine I observed that cats, dogs, cows, and horses, as well as humans, sometimes developed arthritis. Trying to learn why it appeared and to explore the treatment Vermont folk medicine had worked out for the disease, it seemed to me that I ought to have some experimental animals.

The dairy cow appeared to be well adapted for the purpose. Cows and humans are much alike. The period of pregnancy in both is nine months. In Vermont both go into winter quarters in the fall. Both, oddly enough, have increased the tempo of their existence.

Nature intended the cow to make enough milk out of roughage to nourish one calf, but the modern dairy industry expects a cow to make enough milk in her lactation period to nourish eight or ten calves. Humans, with bodies designed for ancient times, are asked to adapt to modern living.

Every human does many more things during the day than he once did. He rides more and walks less. He has less leisure time in which to relax; the pressure of business or professional competition is ever present, and the effort needed to meet the demands of his economic life has increased. The human motor is no longer easily shifted from high to low gear.

Both the dairy cow and man have a long intestinal tract, and both were intended to live on roughage represented by the tender leaves of plants. Because the human's body and that of the cow respond alike to the same fundamental nutritional laws I suspect that in the distant past there was a time when the same food intake satisfied both. They did not live on grains or by-products but fed on foilage, tender leaves of trees and buds, rich grasses, berries, and fruit. A study I made of the Vermont farmer during the warmer months of the year, when he lives close to the soil, showed that he eats the leaves of forty-five plants and bushes and eight different trees.

The cow is an ideal animal for experimental purposes because she is a production animal, producing milk. A reduction in the amount of milk produced is noticed at once, especially if it is weighed at each milking. Any variation in the amount of milk produced forms a valuable check on the health of the animal. When she is slaughtered, the cow also serves as a source of food, and the state of her tissues, whether tender or tough, gives added information.

When we compare the feeding habits of wild animals with existing methods of feeding domesticated animals it is apparent that our whole scheme of feeding needs revision. The animals in our forests do not live on grains or by-products. They feed on foliage and the tender leaves of trees and bushes.

Until fifty years ago no one searched for the reasons why these parts were so nutritious. The seeds of plants contain only what is needed to send their first shoots into the air and their rootlets into the earth. Seeds are low in bone-building minerals and in the elements that regulate animal life processes. Their chief ingredients are starch and oil. Wild animals prefer leaves to seeds.

In the leaves of plants grown in mineral rich surroundings are found the essential mineral compounds for building bones and promoting the growth of body tissues. Seeds or grains have a low mineral content, and the by-products of such grains generally are also of low mineral value. They present, at best, an unbalanced picture, lacking in all-around mineral strength.

Like man's environment, that of the dairy cow has also changed during the passing years. Consider the Jersey cow, for example. By selective breeding the Jersey is now so altered that she finds herself largely a chemical factory, taking in a great amount of hay and grain but not transforming this prodigious amount of fodder into roaming the fields, escaping a mountain lion or a pack of wolves, or journeying to other scenes and other pastures.

The Jersey cow is fed, warmed, sheltered, and protected by man, and her sole activity from birth to death is to be fed, to bear young, and to give milk. The result is that she is very likely to show deterioration. Often one needs to rehabilitate and recondition a Jersey cow, just as a medical man needs to rehabilitate and recondition human individuals who consult him as patients.

As I studied a herd of forty-five registered Jersey cows, it became quite evident that the modern cow is not today the cow of the wild roaming herd. Her calf is not strong at birth. It is often not able to get up on its feet for some time after being born. It has much less hair on its body, and is a fussy calf that is hard to raise. Often aid must be given in order for a Jersey cow to give birth to her calf. Labor is prolonged, instead of being short.

Moreover, calves need increasingly greater care in their growth and maturity. So much calcium goes into the production of milk that there is not enough for the cow to give her offspring. As a result, calves are undersize. I note, too, that the resistance of the Jersey cow to disease seems to be lessening. Just as carrying a heavy pack is hard work, so too is the production of much milk a heavy labor.

For many years the dairy cow has been developed by man through breeding selection, which partly suspends the law of natural selection in the wild. In such natural selection has always been involved the extermination of those that are weakest in muscle and the least fit in the special senses, leaving those with the keenest senses, the fleetest feet, and the most intelligent minds to reproduce their kind.

To domesticate the dairy cow requires considerable thought. Not only must the life of the animal be protected, but living conditions must be provided that will promote health and tranquility. For the dairy cow must thrive and multiply and produce good milk, otherwise domestication will fail.

By following these cows on pasture and studying them in the barn we discover what has been left out that is very much needed in domesticating them. And as we learn this from the cows, so are we able to discern what has been left out by man as he changes the environment in which he lives.

Finally, using the dairy cow as an experimental animal, we learn to understand arthritis better, and what the human body needs to rehabilitate itself and free itself from the disease.

Chapter Nine

Increasing the Bacterial Content of the Body

ONE SPRING my farmer friend planted peas and oats in a six-acre field which had been created by fencing it off with electrified wire. Since it was a new field there were no bushes or trees growing around the edge. It was fertilized with hen manure, which I had learned by testing would make very alkaline anything that grew in the soil.

During the summer my friend planned to turn his herd of fifty-four dairy cows into this field, with the expectation that a great deal of milk would be produced. I asked if I might have the privilege of extracting the juices from the peas and oats and testing their reaction before he turned the herd loose. With no bushes or trees at hand it was certain the cows would eat only the oats and peas.

When I extracted the juices I found them alkaline in reaction, as I had expected, and consequently exactly opposite to what dairy cows sought when they were on pasture, obeying their natural instincts. I asked myself whether the diet of alkaline vegetation would so change the chemistry in the cows' bodies that their tissues would become suitable soil for the growth of harmful germs. Further, I wondered whether the alkaline diet would produce swelling of one or more quarters of the udder in cows with sensitive udders, and produce streptococci germs in the milk.

If these things happened, the indication for treatment, according to Vermont folk medicine, would be to shift the chemistry of the cows' bodies by frequent doses of apple cider vinegar, and to give the cows iodine in the form of Lugol's solution of iodine, which every druggist carries in stock.

At the time the herd was turned into the field all the cows in it were free from mastitis in their udders, and no apple cider vinegar was being used in their feed at the time. But soon, as a result of eating the alkaline peas and oats, seventeen of the fifty-four cows promptly developed mastitis.

On July 5th the bacteriologist at the local creamery reported that the milk delivered there from the herd showed the presence of streptococci germs. The farmer thought a change in pasture, where the cows could get acid vegetation, would clear up the mastitis. It did, in all but eight cows. A bacteriological examination of the milk from these cows showed the presence of streptococci in proportions ranging all the way from one-quarter to the entire udder.

On July 15th, ten days after mastitis was first discovered, the eight remaining afflicted cows were kept in the barn so they could be treated. The first treatment indication was to shift the body chemistry of each of these cows so their tissues would no longer be suitable soil for streptococci germs to grow.

The second treatment was to give each cow Lugol's solution of iodine. I had learned that three drops of iodine in two ounces of apple cider, poured over the ration of each cow, reduced the bacterial content of the pasteurized milk to such an extent that in one herd which had been given the treatment the owner was paid twenty-five cents more for each hundred pounds of milk because of the unusually low bacterial count.

Most of the iodine in a cow's body is held by the thyroid gland. Lugol's solution enables this gland to reduce the virulence of micro-organisms, and eventually to destroy harmful germs every time the blood passes through the gland. Iodine is absorbed so rapidly that the concentration of it in the blood rises to a peak in ninety minutes.

In cows, iodine appears in the milk. Iodine in the blood and iodine eliminated from the cow's body in the milk makes it difficult for streptococci germs to remain.

After we had taken the first two steps in treating the cows there was still a third treatment: lowering the amount of protein intake, a customary procedure in mastitis. All three treatments were applied without delay so that the cows could be cured and returned to the herd as soon as possible.

A timetable for the first two treatments will indicate how they were carried out:

6 A.M. —Each cow was given six ounces of apple cider vinegar and six ounces of water by mouth from a bottle.

8 A.M. —Each cow was given by mouth from a bottle a teaspoonful of Lugol's solution of iodine, plus six ounces of apple cider vinegar and six ounces of water.

10 A.M. —A repetition of the vinegar-and-water dose.

12 NOON—Repeat the dose of vinegar and water.

2 P.M. —A teaspoonful of iodine, and the same dose of vinegar and water.

4 P.M. —Another dose of vinegar and water, same proportions.

7 P.M. —A final dose for the day of vinegar and water.

In addition, two ounces of vinegar were poured over the ration of each cow at the twice daily feedings.

Treatment was begun on July 15th and continued. Every day samples of milk from each affected quarter of the udder were examined by the creamery bacteriologist. On July 18th, after three days of this program, the bacteriologist reported that the milk from all eight cows was free from streptococci in all four quarters of each udder.

In this experiment the entire herd of fifty-four was first used as a group. Later, each cow that did not respond to a change in pasture served as an experimental animal. Naturally, the question we confronted was simply what had been done that should not have been done, and vice versa. How were the diary cows in this herd forced to rebel against nature and desert the animal kingdom? I asked myself what lessons we could learn from this experiment that would help us to understand better how arthritis is produced, and how it might be made less severe and eventually controlled.

First, let us consider the error of commission. Obviously the soil in the field should not have been fertilized with hen manure, insuring that all the vegetation growing there would be alkaline and unsuitable for the cows.

If a dairy cow secretes enough acid in her digestive tract she may overcome the kind of alkaline reaction this herd acquired from eating the peas and oats and so may avoid mastitis. Some of the cows did just that. But if the acid secretion does not occur in a sufficient amount, then the cow's blood becomes more alkaline, with the result that her milk, which is modified blood, loses its normal weakly acid reaction and becomes alkaline. Consequently it is suitable soil for the growth of micro-organisms, and harmful germs make their appearance. In an increased alkaline reaction of the

cow's blood calcium will be precipitated, which makes her
meat tough and tasteless.

By limiting the food intake of the herd to alkaline reaction vegetation the cows had been forced temporarily to
rebel against nature and desert the animal kingdom.

That brings us to the error of omission. Acid intake could
have been increased by giving the herd vinegar with their
feed for a week before turning them into a new pasture which had vegetation not proven safe. It would have
been wise to add three drops of iodine to each two ounces
of vinegar in the feed. In this way the cows could have
been fortified against possible harm from the untried vegetation.

In brucellosis the abortion of calves is promptly stopped
by pouring two ounces of apple cider vinegar containing
three drops of iodine over the ration of pregnant cows at
each feeding twice a day after the ration is placed in the
trough. This shows the effect of iodine and vinegar upon
harmful germs present in the blood.

The effect of iodine is also shown by a very low bacterial
count of the milk. Because we want to eliminate streptococci germs from the milk we use iodine for its effect on
both the blood and the milk.

What lesson, then, can we learn from all this that will
help us to understand better how arthritis is produced, and
how it may be made less severe? Well, we know that it is a
valuable use of time to test the reaction of our food before
it enters our mouths, to make a record of the reaction of
each one so we can study it and use it for future reference.
That study should teach us to eliminate foods that are
found to be alkaline in reaction, otherwise we rebel against
nature. We need to remember that boiling water makes it
alkaline in reaction, and this may change the reaction of
food from what it was before it was boiled.

We should remember, too, that the human body is an acid-
consuming, acid-manufacturing, and acid-eliminating machine, and that the blood is always alkaline because of the
presence in it of sodium bicarbonate, commonly called baking soda. The blood may be more alkaline (hyperalkaline)
or it may be less (hypoalkaline). The normal reaction is
faintly alkaline.

There is a slight difference between the alkaline reaction
of the blood that flows in the veins and in the arteries.
Blood in the veins is a little less alkaline because it con-

tains carbonic acid, resulting from cell activity, which it is carrying to the lungs. The blood in the arteries is a little more alkaline because the carbonic acid leaves the blood as it passes through the lungs.

The reaction of the blood remains remarkably constant in spite of the fact that the activity of the body cells is constantly adding acid to it. Cell activity produces carbonic acid, which produces blood acidity. Use of our muscles results in lactic acid, which also increases acidity as it enters the blood. Scientists estimate that in severe muscular activity lasting only a few minutes as much as ninety grams of lactic acid may be produced. In addition, sulphuric acid and phosphoric acid are the result of cell activity.

In spite of all the carbonic acid, lactic acid, sulphuric acid, and phosphoric acid brought to the blood every day, it remains constantly alkaline in reaction. This is because of the constant pressure of sodium bicarbonate, and the ability of the lungs, kidneys, and skin to remove promptly from the blood any excess of acid that may be present.

When lactic acid, resulting from muscular activity, or phosphoric or sulphuric acid enter the blood they are met at once by the blood's sodium bicarbonate, which is alkaline in reaction. This alkaline sodium bicarbonate is the opposite of the acids represented by lactic, phosphoric, and sulphuric. The sodium bicarbonate converts these into weaker acids, and in this way the effect they would ordinarily have in raising the acidity of the blood is greatly weakened.

The acid chiefly added to the blood as the result of the food burning of body cells is carbonic. Any increase in blood acidity, like that resulting from cell activity, stimulates the breathing center and causes more rapid breathing, with an increased elimination of carbonic acid from the lungs. The kidneys also act as regulators of the balance between alkaline and acid elements in the blood. They play an important part in maintaining the normal alkaline-acid balance of the blood by removing from it any excess acid that may be present.

The skin is another helper in removing acid. When human sweat is produced in an amount sufficient to be collected, it is usually distinctly acid in reaction. This acidity is due mainly to lactic acid and volatile acids. The amount of carbonic acid given off from a man's skin during a twenty-four-hour period varies greatly, but the amount is small unless there is marked sweating, in which case it is noticeably increased.

We can thus readily appreciate that the daily job of the body is to get rid of the acid which results from muscle activity, and the burning of food. At the same time the body must also manufacture acid, and if it does not do so properly there is little work for the sodium bicarbonate in the blood to do in neutralizing acid. The result is that sodium bicarbonate increases in the blood, which then becomes more alkaline than it should.

As a result of this increase the urine becomes alkaline in reaction. The skin changes from its normal acid reaction to alkaline. Even the breath becomes less acid. In that way the stage is set for the appearance of sickness, because the disease producing germs grow on an alkaline soil.

Wheat foods, white sugar, milk as a beverage, muscle meats like beef, lamb, and pork, citrus fruits and their juices—all these raise the alkalinity of the blood in the majority of people I have observed in Vermont. This is shown by their ability to shift the urine reaction from acid to alkaline and to produce an alkaline skin reaction. Weather changes toward the cold side and emotional upsets also increase the alkalinity of the blood.

Once an individual understands that he gets sick because he has permitted his body to rebel against nature and become alkaline rather than acid, thus providing the soil for disease, he will shift his food selection. He will take two teaspoonfuls of apple cider vinegar and two teaspoonfuls of honey in a glass of water at each meal, and also eat sour relishes at mealtime in order to lower the increased alkalinity of the blood, shift the urine, skin, and exhaled breath reaction to the acid side, and in doing so change the body soil so that it no longer is favorable for the development of sickness.

Every twenty-four hours the lungs get rid of the equivalent of twenty to forty liters of normal carbonic acid which, as it leaves, prevents the growth of micro-organisms capable of producing illness in the lungs and upper respiratory tract. In that same twenty-four-hour period the kidneys get rid of fifty to a hundred and fifty cubic centimeters of chloride, sulphate, and phosphate, which are all acid. This acid prevents the growth of harmful germs in the urinary tract.

In order to estimate whether the daily job of manufacturing acid by the body cells is properly done and whether there is work for the sodium bicarbonate in the blood to do, the reactions of the urine and skin are taken.

Urine reaction is measured in the morning, on rising, with the aid of nitrazine paper. When the urine is acid in reaction the paper will turn various shades of yellow; when it is alkaline the paper will be blue. If the body cells are doing properly their daily job of manufacturing acid the kidneys will do their share in removing from the blood any excess acid that may be present, so that when the urine is acid in reaction it is evidence that the cells are working correctly.

But if the urine reaction is alkaline we can be sure the cells are not making enough acid to lower the sodium bicarbonate content of the blood, and that the blood is more alkaline than it should be normally. Since calcium is not held in solution in an alkaline medium, this suggests that free calcium is present in the blood to be deposited in blood vessel walls, bursae, and joints, and may also form stones in the kidney and bladder.

By taking two teaspoonfuls of apple cider vinegar and two of honey in a glass of water several times every day this acid drink substitutes for the acid the body cells should make but do not. It may be taken on rising in the morning and at bedtime, or at a morning coffee break and at teatime in the afternoon. Another way is to take it during each meal.

The vinegar-and-honey drink lowers the sodium bicarbonate in the blood, and the urine reaction will serve as a guide as to how many times a day it should be taken.

I should warn you that it is not always easy to change the urine reaction from alkaline to the normal acid. The body seems to develop chemical habits in much the same manner as it does other habits. Often it takes time to change urine reaction, and it may be a month or six weeks before the alkaline reactions become fewer and the acid reactions increase. Sometimes an even longer period may be necessary. But the vinegar-and-honey treatment is the effort that must be made if we want to return to solution the calcium deposited in unusual places in the body.

In addition to urine reaction, skin reaction should also be taken. To do this, first test water from the cold tap with nitrazine paper. If the paper does not change color the water may be considered neutral in reaction and is suitable to use in taking skin reaction. Next, make an applicator by winding some absorbent cotton around one end of a toothpick. Dip this in the water from the cold tap and apply it to the skin three times so that it makes a wet place large enough to moisten the strip of nitrazine paper. Apply the strip and pat it into place with the unwound end of the toothpick. Allow it to remain in place until it is thoroughly moistened, then remove and examine the color. It will be yellow, showing that the skin is acid, or else some shade of blue, showing that it is alkaline.

If the skin is acid in reaction it demonstrates that it is doing its part in removing acid from the blood. If it is alkaline it shows that not enough acid is coming into the blood to lower its sodium bicarbonate. This is another indication that the vinegar-and-honey drink should be taken with every meal, or at other times during the day.

One note of warning to these tests: If the urine reaction is taken after eating food it will generally be alkaline.

Chapter Ten

Decreasing the Bacterial Content of the Body

IN A HERD OF DAIRY COWS I studied, there was turned over to me for experimentation a Jersey cow eight years old, weighing eight hundred pounds. This cow had been purchased when she was two years old, and the owner had become very fond of her. Until two years before she had been a good producer of milk and a profitable cow, but she had developed a chronic mastitis which the owner had hoped to clear up with the continued use of sulfanilamide.

During the previous summer this cow had suffered from mastitis in her udder through the whole season. Every time her milk was examined by the creamery bacteriologist streptococci germs were found. Since there had been no diminishing of the germs the owner had begun to conclude reluctantly that her usefulness to the herd had ended and she would have to be slaughtered for beef. First, however, he agreed to let me experiment with her.

I applied the familiar remedy of Vermont folk medicine, pouring two ounces of apple cider vinegar over her ration after it had been placed in the feed trough. The first time I did this she sniffed at it a few times and then ate it. After she had cleaned up her ration she spent a half-hour licking the trough, apparently to get all the vinegar she could.

I got in touch with the bacteriologist, and after explaining to him what I was doing and why I asked if he would be willing to examine the milk from this cow every three days for the presence of streptococci germs so that I could determine whether the vinegar ration had any influence on the germs. He said he would be glad to coöperate, and at the end of two weeks he reported that an examination of the milk from all four quarters of the cow's udder showed the milk to be free from streptococci. Her chronic mastitis cleared up and never returned during the three years I observed her. She continued to get the vinegar with her rations.

We began adding the vinegar in October. When she gave birth to a calf and started a new lactation period she surprised her owner by giving fifty-five pounds of milk a day. Apple cider vinegar will increase the amount of milk a cow gives, as I have noted before. As a cow's lactation period progresses, there will be no drop in milk production —indeed, the amount often increases.

Because of my success with the Jersey the farmer turned over to me a cow, somewhat larger and of mixed breed. She was mostly Guernsey, with Jersey comprising whatever remained. Here was another cow with chronic mastitis in her udder and streptococci germs in her milk at every examination. The owner said he had decided to sell her for beef because, at least until now, he did not believe the mastitis could be cured. He gave me permission to try any experiment I wished. If I killed her at least we would learn what not to do. If she was still alive after the experiment he could sell her for beef, and if I cleared up her chronic mastitis she would be worth much more than the beef price as a milk producing cow.

As I prepared to experiment I reflected that mastitis in a cow's udder and arthritis in a joint of the human body had always seemed to me to have several things in common. Swelling and inflammation in one or more quarters of a cow's udder and the same manifestation from arthritis in a human both seemed to be manifestations of an interference in chemical and physiological processes in the body which prevented the attainment of normal goals.

The result of this block, I surmised, was a chemical and physiological disintegration, with swelling, inflammation, and bacterial growth. What I wanted to attempt with my experimental cow was to clear up her mastitis and eradicate the streptococci in her milk. Then I wanted to try by every means I could think of to produce a return of mastitis, with the accompanying streptococci, and learn whether a daily continuance of the vinegar treatment would prevent me from doing so. If I could not I would feel that I understood nature's medical reasoning better, and I could approach the problem of arthritis in humans with increased confidence.

I told my farmer friend I appreciated the opportunity he had given me, and said I thought we might learn something of value that would help whenever mastitis appeared in the herd, and in addition we might learn something which would be very helpful to me in the practice of medicine. I said I didn't expect to kill the cow. He could still slaughter her for beef.

Once more I enlisted the help of the creamery bacteriologist and told him what I intended to do, asking if he would examine the milk from each quarter of the udder at frequent intervals to find out what progress I was making. Again he promised his coöperation, but he remarked that he didn't think it was fair to me to experiment on this particular cow, which he knew well as a troublemaker in the herd. She was so badly infected with mastitis, he said, that in his opinion she was beyond help from anyone. I ought to take a cow in which there was at least a fifty-fifty chance of improvement, he concluded. I assured him I didn't mind, and if he would help I was certain I could learn something of value. With that he gave me his blessing.

I assumed supervision of the cow on December 3rd. All four quarters of her udder were swollen. First of all, I advised the addition to her feed of a teaspoonful of apple cider vinegar for every hundred pounds of the cow's one thousand-pound body weight, the mixture to be given at both daily feedings. This meant that as soon as the ration was placed in the feed trough ten teaspoonfuls of undiluted commercial apple cider vinegar, just as it came from the barrel sold by the wholesale grocery company, were poured over the ration from a dish in which the vinegar had been measured.

The cow accepted her ration with the vinegar added, and a half hour after she had cleaned it up she was still licking the trough to get any vinegar that might be left. On December 5th, I asked the farmer to take a sample of milk from each quarter of the udder to be analyzed by the bacteriologist. The report I got then and those in subsequent weeks I set down in journal form as follows:

December 5th—#1 quarter showed the presence of numerous streptococci in the milk. #2 quarter showed a moderate number of streptococci chains present. #3 quarter showed no streptococci present, but the cells were massed in the stained smear. #4 quarter was very bad. The milk from this quarter did not look like milk. Under the microscope the field was crowded with chains of streptococci.

The farmer reported on this date that the cow's udder was a little better. The swelling of the udder was a little less.

December 8th—The farmer reported by telephone that the swelling in three quarters of the udder had gone down, but one quarter was still very swollen. The back quarters, #2 and #3, were down nearly to normal.

December 10th—#1 quarter showed the presence of numerous streptococci in the milk. #2 quarter showed a moderate number of streptococci present. #3 quarter showed no streptococci. #4 quarter was still very bad, with numerous streptococci. A second report at the end of the first week showed no progress had been made in freeing the first, second, and third quarters of the udder from streptococci.

December 14th—Bacteriological reports showed that there were a few streptococci present in #1 and #2 quarters, none at all in #3 quarter, but numerous streptococci still present in #4 quarter.

December 20ih—The farmer reported by telephone to say

that the cow's udder was in the best condition he had seen it since she first developed mastitis. Three of the quarters were now normal in size, and the #4 quarter, which had been in the worst shape, was now seventy-five per cent normal in size. For the first time there were no lumps in the milk, and the cow ate like the others in the herd. Instead of being slaughtered, she showed every promise of again becoming a profitable member of the herd.

December 21st—The bacteriologist called to say he had just examined smears made from the milk of each quarter of this cow's udder and he could report as follows: #1 quarter, normal milk with no streptococci; #2 quarter, same result, although both this quarter and #1 had showed streptococci only a week before; #3 quarter, continuing to show normal; and #4 quarter, the worst affected of all, only a trace of streptococci present, although a week ago there had been numerous germs, and the milk from this quarter now looked like real milk.

A week ago, said the bacteriologist, he had thought this cow was beyond hope and could not be saved. Now he was sure she could become a profitable and useful member of the herd again.

December 22nd—The farmer reported that the cow continued to show improvement in the amount of milk given by each quarter. Number three quarter, especially, gave a great deal of milk.

December 23rd—When this cow was started on her treatment the hair on her body was rough and she looked dumpish. Now, so the farmer told me, the hair on her body was smooth and looked like the hair of a normal cow. Ever since she had begun to get the vinegar treatment she had licked the cement of her feed trough every time for about a half hour after the ration was cleaned up.

December 27th—I asked the farmer to send a sample of milk from each quarter of the cow's udder for a bacteriological examination at the creamery. The report showed all four quarters to be without any streptococci. All were giving normal milk.

January 3rd—Another bacteriological examination of the

milk from all four quarters of the cow's udder showed them all free of streptococci. The bacteriologist congratulated me on the result. He said he had not thought it was possible to get such a result, especially from such a simple treatment. My farmer friend, of course, was highly pleased. He had five other cows in the herd suffering from mastitis. The udder of each of these cows was returned to normal by giving them the same treatment I had given my experimental animal.

The farmer's reaction to the experiment was that we had learned a great deal, and he suggested we continue to experiment on the cows and try to learn more. I suggested that we try a different approach and attempt to give the animal mastitis while we continued the apple cider vinegar treatment, in the same manner as before. From this procedure we would be able to learn whether streptococci would return to the milk. We decided to work her hard by increasing the protein content of her ration and by giving her a place in the barn that had been occupied by a cow which had suffered from mastitis. Later we placed her near the door opening into the stable so that she would be subject to drafts.

January 5th—The cow continued to hold up well. No mastitis had appeared. Protein was being increased to find out how much of it she could take before mastitis made its appearance. She was now getting as much protein as any producing cow in the herd.

January 7th—The strip cup, which has a fine meshed screen across its top, showed that the milk from #3 quarter, formerly the best one, contained a few flakes. This quarter was swollen a little in the morning, but at noon the swelling had disappeared and for the moment there were no flakes in the milk.

January 8th—The cow was normal in all four quarters of her udder, as shown by the strip cup. She was not being favored, but was getting sixteen per cent protein in her ration.

January 10th—The cow's udder continued to be free from mastitis, and she was the only one in the herd getting sixteen per cent protein. The remainder of the cows got a fourteen per cent protein ration, because at the moment the hay being fed to the herd was very rich in protein. But in spite of the experimental cow's high protein ration, her udder remained normal.

January 18th—No change in the normal condition of the cow's udder. The bacteriologist from the creamery called to tell me that the milk from all four quarters of the udder was still free from streptococci and showed normal milk.

January 20th—From December 26th until this date we had tried to produce mastitis in the cow's udder while she was getting her vinegar twice a day, but we could not bring back the disease.

February 28th—I suggested that the cow be sold to a nearby cattle dealer so that we might learn what happened to her when it was not known she needed vinegar with her ration. At the time she was sold she had just started a new pregnancy. The dealer who bought her did not, of course, give her the vinegar treatment and in due time she once more developed mastitis. As a result, two quarters of her udder finally gave no milk at all. The dealer dried her off and turned her out to pasture for the summer, thinking she would get over her disease. When she gave birth to her calf in the fall she gave milk from only two quarters of her udder. That made her an unprofitable cow, and she was sold for beef.

I believe this may be the place to summarize my observations, of which the dairy cow experiment was the logical culmination. As I studied native Vermonters, living close to the soil, I had noted how the vinegar-and-honey treatment at each meal contributed to their continued good health and freedom from sickness. From a two-year study of twelve adults and twelve little children who had acted as human guinea pigs I had learned that sickness appeared on an alkaline urine reaction background, and recovery from sickness came when the urine reaction changed to the normal acid reaction and continued to be acid.

I had learned from reading medical literature that the body cells manufactured carbonic acid, lactic acid, phosphoric acid, and sulphuric acid. These four brought to the blood each day were met by the sodium bicarbonate of the blood, which is alkaline in reaction, and converted them into weaker acids. In this way the effect that these acids had in raising the acidity of the blood was greatly weakened. If these four acids were not manufactured by body cells in suitable amounts the sodium bicarbonate increased in the blood was not used as it was intended to be. By its alkaline reaction it made body tissues suitable soil for the growth of harmful germs, which naturally grow on an alkaline soil.

Infestation of the body by these germs appeared to be changed into infection through an increase in the sodium bicarbonate content of the blood. The question arose as to whether apple cider vinegar from an organic source like apples would be accepted by the human body as a substitute for the four acids normally manufactured by body cells, but which were not made in suitable amounts because of a biochemical block in the body. Would vinegar made from the whole apple lower the sodium bicarbonate of the blood to the point where an acid urine reaction appeared, and would it continue to be present on rising in the morning and before the evening meal?

I learned from the late Professor Cavanaugh of Cornell that the reaction of a cow's milk varies between an acid reaction of pH 5.8 and 6.2. When the shift to alkaline occurs with an attack of mastitis, accompanied by streptococci germs, the reaction of the milk changes to alkaline pH 7 or to 7.5. Sodium chloride is a neutral salt. It is the sodium bicarbonate, often referred to as baking soda, that shifts the milk reaction of a cow to the alkaline side.

The osmotic pressure of a cow's blood makes it possible for the watery part to pass through the sievelike walls of the tiny blood vessels called capillaries, as ink passes through blotting paper. It is made up of five per cent sugar, .6 plus albumin, and .3 plus salt. The osmotic pressure of the blood in a cow, therefore, is due to sugar, albumin, and salts.

When the natural carbohydrate intake represented by fruit, berries, edible leaves and roots, and edible foliage, with their organic acid and natural sugar content, is not enough to maintain the five per cent sugar in the blood, the albumin and salt content of the cow's blood go up to maintain the osmotic pressure. When the sugar drops this pressure tends to drop, and then the blood albumin and salts go up to raise the pressure automatically.

Sodium bicarbonate is a normal constituent of blood, which gives it a characteristic faintly alkaline reaction above pH 7.0. Normally, by the process called osmosis, sodium bicarbonate does not go through into the milk. When the sugar in the blood drops low enough albumin and salts in the blood go up. A trace of sodium bicarbonate then goes through into milk, which changes the reaction to alkaline.

Now, with these facts in mind, I understand better why Vermont folk medicine combines apple cider vinegar and honey in the same glass of water. Native Vermonters, with an inquiring and analytical mind, worked out by the trial-and-error method of research a combination of two teaspoonfuls of apple cider vinegar and two teaspoonfuls of honey in a glass of water, to be taken at each meal or at other times of the day that were suitable. By this combination the digestion was improved, heartburn and gas formation were less, bowel action was improved, body warmth and energy similarly improved, sensitiveness to cold was less, quick recovery from fatigue took place, endurance increased, and sound sleep at night was an extra dividend.

It became evident to those who used this drink each day that body performance was greatly improved. I concluded that the reason this occurred was because of the vinegar-and-honey combination's ability to increase the vital activity of body cells, reduce the sodium bicarbonate content of the blood, and furnish the sugar necessary to restore the normal osmotic pressure.

The dairy cow that was turned over to me for experimentation provided the opportunity to learn what part apple cider vinegar played in the vinegar-and-honey combination. I discovered, as you have seen demonstrated in my journal, that it had a great deal to do with decreasing the bacterial content of a cow's body, and I concluded that it was a safe and effective remedy to prescribe for patients who wanted freedom from colds, influenza, sinus trouble, and other types of sickness. For the remedy had been proven by Vermont folk medicine and had stood the test of time.

Continued good reports from patients who took the vinegar-and-honey drink disclosed the fact that it discouraged the forces in the human body which produce sickness. This simple drink—which, incidentally, is called "switchel" by elderly Vermonters—ought not to be forgotten, because it works just as well today as it did two hundred years ago. Because of the numerous helpful things it does in the human body, its use as one of the treatment measures when arthritis is present has seemed to me both natural and advisable.

But there was still one more question I had to ask of nature. Could an inorganic acid not derived from fruit be poured over the ration of a dairy cow with the same good results that appeared when apple cider vinegar was used? In order to establish the answer five gallons of phosphoric acid not made from a fruit was purchased. I chose this liquid because cows in the herd liked the grass in the pasture where acid phosphate had been used as a trial fertilizer.

The phosphoric acid was poured over the ration just as the vinegar had been in an experiment which involved ten dairy cows specially selected. The cows accepted the acid, but within two weeks most of them had developed swollen quarters in their udders, with a thickening of the milk and the appearance of flakes and lumps in it.

As soon as this happened, the acid was discontinued and apple cider vinegar was substituted for it. That soon brought a disappearance of the swelling and returned the milk to normal.

With the phosphoric acid we had produced mastitis, which apple cider vinegar prevented. Nature had given her answer, and it was simply that the acid poured over the ration must be an organic acid from fruit that did not prevent chemical and physiologic processes in a cow's body from reaching their normal goals.

Chapter Eleven

Arthritis: an Energy Disease

FOR MANY YEARS organized medicine has used the bacteriological approach to solve clinical problems presented by a patient. In sharp contrast to this laboratory theory of infection is the theory of energy diseases developed by Vermont folk medicine as a result of close association with nature. Organized medicine has come to its hypotheses through the test tube and the microscope; Vermont folk medicine's ap-

proach has been through the study of the instincts and behavior of wild and domesticated fowl and animals.

Folk medicine recognizes three kinds of sickness that may
appear in the human body. The first is referred to as
energy diseases resulting from continued activity of the
energy expending mechanism in the body, because the individual does not know how to release the body from such
activity. In this category would come high blood pressure,
heart attacks, stomach and intestinal ulcer, muscle paralysis,
hay fever, asthma, migraine headaches, diabetes mellitus,
arthritis, and cancer.

The second variety of sickness is what folk medicine calls
bacteriological diseases, caused by the presence within the
body of harmful micro-organisms that grow, multiply, and
destroy. They are often referred to as infectious diseases.
Typhoid fever would be one of them.

The third kind is known as parasitic diseases, or those
due to the bites of insects and the presence within the body
of parasites, like the trichinosis which develops when you
eat contaminated pork containing the parasites of this disease.

As a result of its method of research—the trial-and-error
method—Vermont folk medicine has come to believe that
physiological and chemical changes in the body underlie
modern sickness. These changes are considered to be the
same whether they occur in plants, fowl, animals, or man,
in that they produce clinical physiology and biochemistry in
the body.

The part of the body affected and which tissue or organ
shows a change in function is governed by the ability of
the body cells of that part to resist the altered body physiology and chemistry. Folk medicine reasoning in these mat-
ters is based on observing fowl and animals while they are
alive, and noting what happens after they are slaughtered
and prepared for market.

To understand how this reasoning is applied, let us have
a closer look at the energy expending mechanism. It is
helpful, particularly, for anyone with arthritis to understand
how the mechanism works, because arthritis is considered an
energy disease by folk medicine, and many of its observations, deductions, and conclusions are related to the behavior of that mechanism. It is natural that this should be
so because most of the domesticated fowl and farm animals
are kept for what they will produce, and anything that inter-

feres with normal production is of interest to the owner.

To begin with it is well known that only certain organs and tissues control the expenditure of energy in all animals, including man. As we have enumerated before these are the brain, heart, blood, the thyroid gland, the adrenal glands, the celiac ganglia, and the sympathetic division of the autonomic nervous system. The adrenal glands govern emergency energy, while the thyroid controls the level of constant energy. Taken together, these organs and tissues are the means whereby energy is released in this or that gland or combination of muscles to enable an animal or human being to secure food, to escape from danger, and to reproduce its kind.

The transmitting system of animals and man includes the sensory nerves of the body, the nerves that control the voluntary muscles, and the sympathetic nerves that supply the great network of blood vessels, which in turn are supplied to each of the hundreds of millions of cells of the liver, the thyroid gland, and the digestive system.

These energy controlling systems constitute a network so vast and intricate that if all the tissues of the body were removed except the nerve mechanisms there would remain only an effigy. Standing alone without accelerators or controllers these mechanisms would work all day and night, in danger, in hunger, in the presence of prey or mates. But it would be of little benefit to man or to animals like the race horse to have a perfect mechanism for generating energy if there were no compensating device by which speed could be adaptively altered.

In such a hypothetical situation man would not be able to adapt his mechanism to his changing requirements. The race horse would not be able to develop his speed. Man and all animals would exist on a constant energy level; they would operate at a given speed and their energy would be changeless. The mating season would be identical with every other season, and there would be no rhythm of adaptation to cold.

Thus, if every animal had the same speed of energy transformation everything would be alike and predictable. There would be only basic oxidation, not adaptive oxidation. The ovaries, testes, mammary glands, muscles, bones, tendons, the fat, and connective tissues—none of these can alone change the rate of burning food in the cells of the body. The brain can supply the spark to start food burning which results in the production of energy, but it cannot adaptively regulate the speed with which the burning of food in the body cells takes place without the help of the heart, the adrenal-sympathetic nervous system, and the special senses.

The brain-heart-thyroid-adrenal-sympathetic system represents the energy expending mechanism of the body, and is the distinguishing feature of man and the higher animals. It controls adaptively the muscular action, glandular secretion, and emotional expression.

When we make a supreme effort all the available energy is mobilized. Adrenalin circulating through the blood stream causes a flash of oxidation not only in the millions of brain cells but in the entire sympathetic nervous system. Cells and system are stimulated at the same time to their maximum activity.

This simultaneous stimulation of the adrenal glands, the celiac ganglia and plexuses, and the sympathetic nervous system causes a powerful beat of the heart, a speeding of the sugar from the liver to the blood stream, and a speed-up of breathing. The result is a great output of energy for attack that more nearly resembles an explosion than a physiological act. Following such a maximum amount of activity there is rapid exhaustion. All the processes of the body not needed in the emergency are meanwhile completely prohibited.

Let us observe how this mechanism works, beginning with the body at rest. That part of the nervous, endocrine, and chemical systems which builds up and stores reserves against the day of need is now in the driver's seat. The whole process of food intake and digestion, from the moment of a desire to eat down to the evacuation of indigestible residue, is under its control. Now the door of each body cell is readily opened to allow food and oxygen derived from the blood stream to enter, so that the vital activity of the cell may be carried on. The fluid in the body derived from the blood stream is constantly on the move, on its way to the body cells which are ready to receive it. There is no gathering of unwanted fluid by the cells in any part of the body.

In this state of bodily rest the heartbeat and breathing are at a relatively slow rate. The larger part of the blood supply has been withdrawn from the brain, muscles, heart, and lungs and placed at the disposal of the digestive tract and abdominal organs, which are quietly engaged in carrying on the vital processes of the body. That part of the nervous system which brings about peace and quiet in the body is in control, and the portion of the endocrine system designed to increase the ability of the body cells to take up fluid laden with food and oxygen is active. The human motor is in low gear.

Then an alarm is sounded. Any one of the five senses, but usually sight, hearing, or touch, brings a warning of impending danger, and at once that part of the nervous, endocrine, and chemical mechanism which organizes the body for an emergency takes over. Heart and breathing speed up rapidly to hasten the circulation of blood and to meet the increased need for oxygen taken in by the lungs and transferred to the blood. In the digestive tract and abdominal organs blood is drained to be sent to the muscles, brain, eyes, ears, and heart. Each adrenal gland is activated, and through the emergency function they possess, they pour adrenalin into the blood stream, which serves to increase and prolong the activity of the nervous and chemical systems that organize the individual for combat. The heartbeat is strengthened, and the blood is suffused with sugar stored in the liver, glands, and muscles.

To produce the display of energy needed to meet an emergency when an alarm is sounded, the human motor is now in high gear. These changes characterize the new state:

1. There is a cessation of processes in the digestive tract.
2. Blood shifts from the abdominal organs to the organs immediately essential to muscular exertion.
3. There is increased vigor of contraction of the heart.
4. A discharge of extra blood corpuscles from the spleen occurs.
5. There is deeper breathing.
6. A dilation of the breathing tubes leading to the lungs takes place.
7. There is a quick abolition of muscular fatigue and mobilizing of sugar in the circulation.

When war breaks out between nations the arts and industries that brought wealth and contentment must suffer serious neglect or be wholly set aside by both attacker and attacked. All the supplies and energies developed in the period of peace must be devoted to the present conflict.

So it is with the body. Functions which establish and support the body reserves in a quiet time are, in time of stress, instantly checked or completely stopped, and these reserves are drawn upon lavishly to increase power in attack or defense.

There are lesser demands made on the nervous, endocrine, and chemical mechanisms that organize the body for varying degrees of great effort—demands like fear, anxiety, unproductive worry, an unhappy environment, grief, a drop in the outdoor temperature, and certain foods. These factors, which are present singly or in combination in some degree every day, maintain the body on one of the varying levels of emergency organization. The body cells are denied the proper quantity and quality of food they need to build up body reserves.

Doctors who are called upon to treat modern man recognize that his peaceful intervals are few and far between. As he lives his business and private life he inevitably encounters recurring frustrations and irritations, and the emotions of fear, anger, anxiety, joy, grief, and deep disgust.

Under primitive conditions the body's device for mobilizing its energy expending mechanism for fight or flight was probably of major importance, but today it is likely to be more detrimental than otherwise. Emergencies in these days most commonly call for self-control and quiet thinking. Nevertheless, these primitive reactions constantly take place, with results somewhat comparable to opening the throttle of an idling motor.

The effect on the machinery is not wholesome. When we are overwrought it would probably be wise if we did something vigorous, not commit an assault, of course, but take a brisk walk in order to use the body as it was intended to be used when organized for an emergency. When the body goes on a combat basis the physiological changes that suddenly occur are all adapted to putting forth a supreme muscular and nervous effort, because primitive battle consisted of fierce physical combat of beast with beast, man with man, or one against the other.

Many surface manifestations are easily observable when the body organizes itself on a combat basis. They are present in a degree measured by the intensity with which the organization takes place. These manifestations include contraction of blood vessels, with resulting pallor; the pouring out of cold sweat; stopping of saliva flow; dilation of the pupils of the eyes; rising of the hairs; a rapid beating of the heart; hurried respiration; trembling and twitching of the muscles, especially those about the lips.

Such signs and symptoms are all well recognized accompaniments of pain and great emotional disturbances such as horror, anger, and deep disgust, but they are mainly superficial. There are other organs hidden deep in the body which do not display so obviously the disturbance of their action during states of intense feeling.

As an organ of struggle the mind of man keeps his energy expending mechanism constantly under the stress of fear, worry, and anxiety. As a result a group of clinical conditions peculiar to civilized man have appeared, which might be called energy diseases.

The heart of modern man is affected profoundly by the frettings and frustrations peculiar to his way of life—a pattern in which he works physically, mentally, and emotionally all day and worries at night. Man is a combat animal and will probably always be one. It is this combat instinct that makes business and professional competition attractive to him. The way of living he has created will not wreck him, however, if he learns how to control the energy expending mechanism of his body.

You may ask, "Why should an individual with arthritis be interested in this mechanism?" He should be interested because conditions in his life may be responsible for activating the energy expending mechanism, and he ought to know what happens in the body in relation to arthritis when that activation occurs.

He should know, for example, that a change in the reaction of the blood takes place, its normal faintly alkaline reaction increasing until it becomes hyperalkaline. Then the blood calcium is precipitated, just as it is in the teakettle when the water boils, and precipitated calcium forms a deposit, just as it does on the bottom of the teakettle.

This free calcium in the blood makes the body tissues tough, interferes with the normal formation of tissue juices, makes it more difficult for the heart to circulate the blood, and brings about a deposit of calcium in the blood vessel walls. When the body holds all the precipitated calcium possible it spills over into the bursae and the joints.

The object of treatment is to throw the deposited calcium into solution again, thus relieving joints and bursae of the precipitated calcium. Dairy cows in pasture achieve this, as we have seen, by selecting only acid reaction vegetation, and native Vermonters do it by the daily use of apple cider vinegar on their food and by taking honey. By using the vinegar-and-honey combination the daily food intake is made acid in reaction before it enters the mouth, in accordance with nature's plan. This prevents calcium from precipitating in the body. One reason why these Vermonters live so long is their ability to solve the calcium problem. They keep body tissues free from deposits in places where no deposits should occur.

It is common knowledge that arthritic patients feel worse when they are under some emotional strain which activates their energy expending mechanism. In some an emotional upheaval can produce an attack of arthritis, and in all of them the mechanism may be activated by such common emotional problems as chronic resentment, an unhappy marriage, a bitter career disappointment, or by some frustration against which the person battles subconsciously every day. The first symptoms of arthritis may occur immediately after a siege of family trouble, and it will be caused by mineral precipitation in the body which activates the energy expending mechanism.

A common illustration from Vermont daily life will illustrate, I think, what happens when the mechanism is set in motion. During the deer season if a deer is shot while it is calmly eating or resting, with its body motor in low gear, the cooked meat will be very tender and have a good taste. But if he is frightened, shifts his body motor into high gear and starts running, and is shot while running, the cooked meat will be tough and have a poor taste. That is a homely but vivid example of what happens when the energy expending mechanism is dominant. As I have said before, native Vermonters have learned that they can throw the precipitated calcium into solution and make the meat of fowl or animals tender and good tasting by a twice-a-day apple cider vinegar dose before the animal is slaughtered.

It is a paradox in our modern world that nearly every machine you can buy is accompanied by a book of instructions telling you how to operate it and make simple adjustments, but the human machine, as old as man himself, has never had any such instructions, except those which medicine has provided. We are, however, born with instincts which nature intended to guide and protect us. Leaving these instincts behind us in childhood and denying them later we lose the knowledge that enables us to shift from high to low gear. Yet is quite possible to relearn this knowledge.

A young Vermonter learns it by demonstrating how it is possible to calm down a cross dog, an irritable horse, or a pugnacious bull, simply by adding apple cider vinegar to the animal's ration at each feeding each day and repeating this daily for a month or two.

When I heard about this treatment from my native Vermont friends it aroused my interest at once, because it indicated that this was a way to shift the human motor from high to low gear. I spent five years in studying pugnacious bulls to find out whether the sweetening of the disposition was accurate or not.

The owner of the herd I studied did not raise his replacements but purchased them from cattle dealers and nearby farmers. Consequently he classified the bulls in his herd as animals to be sold for beef when they were ready for market.

It was only logical, then, that when the farmer bought a bull his first thought was to put some weight on him and his second thought was to make the meat tender. The bulls were therefore always in rotation in the herd: as soon as one was properly conditioned for a profitable sale another was bought to take his place.

Some of the bulls, by the law of averages, were short-tempered animals, which is probably one of the reasons why they were sold. They would bellow, wave their heads from side to side, and paw the barn floor. To put it conservatively, they were entirely out of harmony with the barn environment. I asked permission to try out apple cider vinegar on these bulls to learn whether it would control their dispositions.

A pint of apple cider vinegar, just as it came from the vinegar barrel, was placed before a belligerent bull to study his reaction. He sniffed it a few times and then took all of it. Then we put a quart before him, and he took it quickly without any ill effects. Apparently apple cider vinegar is acceptable to a bull, because he will take a large amount of it if he is given a chance. Repeated trials with various bulls showed that every one would take a pint of vinegar any time it was placed before him.

I learned that any pugnacious bull could be calmed down simply by pouring two ounces of apple cider vinegar over his ration at each feeding. In time, if the treatment was continued, he would become docile and could be easily handled, although I might add that he was never to be trusted.

After five years of calming down bulls by this method I asked my farmer friend what he thought of it. "Dr. Jarvis," he said, "we don't have any cross bulls in this barn any more."

Turning to humans, in the practice of medicine, I discovered that two teaspoonfuls of vinegar and two of honey in a glass of water would shift the human motor from high to low, and in the process it would calm down the individual and make him easier to live with.

The person with arthritis should try to remember that apple cider vinegar, besides the other results it may produce, will also calm down the energy expending mechanism that organizes the body for aggressive action, either mental or physical. In doing this it shifts the motor from high to low, and since arthritis is an energy disease this knowledge can be very helpful.

Chapter Twelve

The Usefulness of Lugol's Solution of Iodine

A YOUNG VERMONTER not only learns about the virtues of apple cider vinegar, but he is also taught the value of Lugol's solution of iodine, which was devised in the nineteenth century by a French physician.

At one time I enlisted the aid of twelve small children, none of them more than five years old, who were to serve as human guinea pigs for two years, so that the second year might be compared with the first year. The object of this study was to learn whether little children got sick on an alkaline urine or an acid urine reaction background. In time I learned that they did indeed become ill on the alkaline reaction and recovered when the urine was restored to its normal acid reaction.

There were twins in this group of children, and their

mother said to me, "Dr. Jarvis, what am I going to do? One of these girls is a race horse and the other is a farm horse. I mean that one is nervous, high-strung, and irritable and won't accept discipline. She's always ready to fight. But the other one has a calm, even disposition; she's so peaceful and quiet. My problem is that the race horse twin keeps both her calm sister and me stirred up all the time. It doesn't do any good to spank her because she just blows up and I have a worse problem on my hands. Tell me, how are we going to live with this girl?"

"Let's turn to Vermont folk medicine," I said, "and use Lugol's solution of iodine to release the continued activity of the energy expending mechanism in her body. Any time her motor shifts into high and she shows the increased speed by becoming a discipline problem, add a teaspoonful of apple cider vinegar to a glass of water in order to make the water in the glass acid in reaction. Then add two drops of Lugol's solution of iodine to the glass of water, and after the mixture is stirred have her drink it. Give it to her whenever she seems to need it to get into low gear. It can be done anytime during the day, at meals or between meals."

Two weeks later the mother reported that her race horse daughter quieted down within two hours after the dosage I had recommended was given, and with the continued help of the solution she was able to control the child easily. Sometimes she gave it every day if it seemed to be needed, or at longer intervals if there were no outbursts.

Today the twin who was treated is married and in her own home. With the aid of iodine-and-vinegar during her growing years her human motor was brought under control and she developed into a normal girl. By the time she graduated from high school the tantrums of her childhood were only a memory. But if she ever becomes high-strung and irritable again, she will know the remedy.

I recall another child whose mother was a professor in a college for women before her marriage to a man who was a university graduate. Their first child, a girl, had an even disposition and was easy to live with, but their second, another girl, was the kind of race horse type I have just discussed. The mother came to me with the same complaint as the harassed mother of twins, and again I suggested the same folk medicine remedy of iodine and vinegar. Once more the treatment worked perfectly. The mother gave me an almost identical report: within two hours her daughter was a different child.

As time passed, this girl too developed into a normal high school student and was later extremely successful in college, where she developed her really fine mind and her artistic abilities, as well as the ability she had acquired to get along with others and make friends.

Two drops of Lugol's solution of iodine works equally well in an adult. When the stress and strain of daily living create a load that is difficult to carry, producing a state of anxiety, and when the day's problems make it difficult to relax and sleep well at night, then one appreciates the aid that iodine gives.

In an adult two teaspoonfuls of apple cider vinegar and two of honey are added to a glass of water. The honey is there because it is a sedative. Then add two drops of Lugol's solution of iodine to the glass containing the vinegar-and-honey mixture, stir it, and sip it during the meal as you would coffee or tea. Taken apart from the meal it can be sipped like a cocktail. Soon your motor will have slipped into low gear. Your problems and their solution will seem less difficult, and the day's load of responsibility easier to carry. In this age of anxiety the combination of iodine with vinegar and water will give the harassed individual increased energy and the endurance necessary to carry the daily load. You will find that the wear and tear of daily living is considerably reduced.

The same remedy can be applied to cattle, in a somewhat different way than I have already described in the treatment of mastitis, although in the example I have in mind the reason for administering it was the same. My farmer friend called me one day to inform me that four of his best cows were sick with acute mastitis of their udders. The veterinarian had been using the bacteriological approach, employing sulfa drugs, but without success. He had just left the barn, said the farmer, telling him that the cows were going to die. Could I save them?

I told him that attacking bacteria as a solution to medical problems had not always proved successful, as far as I was concerned, and I recommended that we try Vermont folk medicine, seeking to release the energy expending mechanism from its continued activity.

My plan was to change the physiology and chemistry of each cow's body by giving her morning, noon, and night a "blood wash," as folk medicine expresses it. We would give each cow by mouth from a bottle four ounces of apple cider vinegar, four ounces of water, and a teaspoonful of Lugol's solution, all mixed together.

Before the treatment was applied, these cows were running temperatures as high as 107 degrees. After it was given, the fever began to drop at once, and by the end of the week all four had recovered from their sickness. Three of the cows returned to milk production. The fourth did not produce milk until her next calf was born and a new lactation period was started.

The folk medicine approach—that is, releasing the energy expending mechanism from continued activity by giving a "blood wash"—works if sickness with an accompanying elevation of temperature is present in a human. Often a single teaspoonful of vinegar in a glass of water with two drops of iodine added will cause the body temperature to drop when the solution is taken morning, noon, and evening. Continued use often brings rapid recovery from sickness.

When you take Lugol's solution you are taking an excellent catalyst which has the ability to start, and continue at a rapid pace, physiological and chemical processes within the body that would not otherwise begin, or if begun, would proceed at a slow pace. Iodine increases the rapidity of the start, and the rate of speed as well. By means of a catalyst the individual is able to control the internal environment and bring peace to the body.

If a harmful virus or micro-organism is among the factors which cause arthritis Lugol's solution of iodine will be helpful. In the herd of diary cows I studied, I decreased the bacteria content of the milk markedly, as I have shown previously, by adding three drops of iodine to two ounces of vinegar, the whole poured over the ration of each cow at every feeding twice a day.

For pasteurized milk, I might add, a count of five thousand bacteria in each cubic centimeter of milk is acceptable to the creamery laboratory. With the addition of vinegar and iodine to the ration the bacteria count dropped to less than a thousand and did not rise. Often it was five hundred or less.

Chapter Thirteen

The Two Blood Vessel Beds

It is HELPFUL to someone who has arthritis if he has a working knowledge of the two blood vessel beds in the body. Knowledge of them came to folk medicine as Vermont farmers, slaughtering their animals for market and studying the color of the meat and the whiteness of the tallow, came to the conclusion that there was not enough blood in the animal body to fill all the blood vessels at the same time.

They taught young Vermonters, therefore, that the human body has three floors. The ground floor contains the digestive tract and other abdominal organs. The second holds the lungs and heart; while the top floor shelters the brain, and the senses of smell, sight, and hearing which keep an individual in touch with his environment.

In these three floors are two beds made up of blood vessels of various sizes, from the largest to the smallest. One of these beds is located on the ground floor, the abdomen, while the other is on the second and top floors of the body.

The young Vermonter is also taught that there are three trees in the body. One is the digestive tree, with its roots in the stomach. The second is the blood vessel tree, with its roots in the heart; while the third is the nerve tree, whose roots are in the brain. In order to nourish these trees suitably it is necessary that the blood mass in the body be able to shift from one blood vessel bed to the other, changing back and forth according to the nutritional needs of the three trees, and as the body needs may require, whether the need is fight or flight or the normal activity of storing reserves against the day of need.

The blood vessel bed on the second and top floors supplies such tissues as heart, lungs, central nervous system, eyes, ears, the lining of the nose and throat, and the muscles of the arms, legs, and body trunk. On the ground floor the bed there supplies skin, stomach, intestines, liver, spleen, and kidneys. Muscles, brain, and lungs comprise what we call the blood lakes of the second and top floors, while the ground floor lakes are the skin, liver, and spleen.

When food is taken and digestion and absorption are necessary the blood mass in the body shifts from the second and top floor blood vessel bed to the ground floor bed. As it leaves the upper floors the diameter of all the tiny blood vessels, called capillaries, in the bed are lessened in size. This means that less blood carrying food material and oxygen, which body cells need to carry on their vital activity, reach these cells.

As a result of the lessened blood supply the body cells supplied by the second and top floor bed develop a nutritional need which is supplied by shifting the blood mass from the ground floor upward, as soon as it is possible to do so. When the mass leaves the ground floor the diameter of the capillaries is lessened, and in time the cells in this bed develop a nutritional need of their own, which is supplied in turn by a shift of the blood mass back to the ground floor.

We have, then, a balance existing between the two beds. On the flexibility of this balance depends its usefulness. The increase and decrease in the size of the capillaries is changing constantly from one bed to another.

Shifting of the blood mass permits the maintenance of a higher level of body cell activity in one or the other of the beds, depending on whether body demands are for muscular work or for digestive uses. But if the shift of the mass does not take place readily, in accordance with body cell needs, the cells in one bed or the other rebel against the uncongenial environment which fails to furnish them with nourishment.

The result is that the individual becomes body conscious and recognizes that a certain part of the body is not behaving as it normally should. In nervously unstable people the balance between the beds is of great importance; they make the shift of the blood mass frequently and suddenly.

All our lives we must deal with a rhythm of increase and decrease in the size of the capillaries in these two vascular beds. Fundamentally the rhythm depends on the environmental factors present. When you shift the human motor into high gear you shift your blood mass from the ground floor bed to the second and top flood bed, in order to organize for aggressive action. Going into low gear the shift of blood is from top to bottom, to organize the body for peace and quiet and the building of reserves.

As a result of present-day stress and strain and the processing of many foods that we eat there is often an habitual constriction of the capillaries on the ground floor bed, and an increase in capillary size on the upper levels. Outward evidence of the blood mass's fixation on the second and top floor bed is the presence of a continued high blood pressure reading.

To break this fixation and restore a working balance between the upper and lower levels so that a greater part of the blood mass will shift back and forth as needed, Vermont folk medicine first prescribes a high natural carbohydrate food intake—that is, fruits, berries, leafy vegetables, root vegetables—and a low protein intake represented by milk, eggs, cheese, meat, fish, poultry, and seafood.

With this done, four simple remedies are prescribed. They are apple cider vinegar, honey, Lugol's solution of iodine, and kelp tablets. In combination they have a long record of success in breaking up the habit of locking the blood mass in the second and top floor blood vessel bed.

Chapter Fourteen

The Body Pendulum

VERMONT FOLK MEDICINE teaches that within the body there is a pendulum that swings from side to side, like one of the stately grandfather clocks seen everywhere in New England. As we study the shift of the blood mass from a state of peace and quiet to one of emergency and back again, we recognize that this is a chemical and physiological pendulum. Our concern is to see that the pendulum, as it swings from side to side, does not get stuck at some point in its swing and produce sickness.

The constant swinging of the pendulum becomes apparent as an individual lives from day to day. All of us know how that feels. One day we feel peppy, the next sluggish. One day you are "on top of the world," as we put it, but next day we may be in a mood of bleak depression. Here we can recognize easily the pendulum's swing, reflecting the state of the nervous, endocrine, and chemical mechanisms that control his body. These mechanisms change with the seasons, consequently the reaction of the individual to disease producing factors changes from day to day and from season to season. When it is disturbed, the human body seeks to reëstablish an equilibrium. We should not interfere with that process.

We do not learn easily to think of the body in terms of motion. We are more likely to think of it as a fixed unit instead of visualizing it in its true state of increasing movement, with a constant change in form and incessant adaptability—now advancing, now retreating; now stimulated, now quiescent.

Once we begin to think of cells in that way we can get a proper perspective of the body itself as something in constant motion paced by the chemical and physiological swing of the pendulum, which is influenced markedly by the energy load the body is asked to carry. A disease process, especially an acute one, is really like a fast-moving train. One has to hurry to deal with it in a satisfactory manner.

Vermont folk medicine does not concern itself so much with the full development of sickness as it does with the finer beginnings, when the disease stages are in a fluid state and consequently more influenced by suitable treatment. Folk medicine believes that the first symptoms of a sickness appear when the body pendulum comes to rest in some phase of its swing.

Environmental changes are such an everyday affair that we give them only passing attention ordinarily. Folk medicine gives them much more, because it is based on chemical and physiological medicine, and so is very much interested in the swing of the pendulum and how it is influenced by environmental changes. Failure in the swing manifests itself as illness. The cause of the disease makes no difference, whether endocrine, infectious, traumatic, congenital, or a deficiency of some kind. In any case the greater energy demand made upon the body interferes with the swing of the pendulum, and thus the illness is brought into focus.

According to folk medicine, we experience a state of health and well being as long as our complicated organic mechanisms are able to maintain a working equilibrium. All organic functions in the body are constantly undergoing a rhythmic pendulation, because we must maintain our balance in the face of innumerable energy impacts which reach us from the skin, mucous membranes, the gastrointestinal tract, the lungs, or the special sense organs.

No simple change in any organic balance can occur without involving practically all the other balances. The influence of various environmental factors on these balances is like the waves which appear if a stone is thrown into the quiet waters of a pool. The pendulation continues until an equilibrium is reached.

By studying the systolic blood pressure the swing of the biologic pendulum is easily observed. There is characteristic blood pressure reaction to any environmental impact upon the body, such as cold, emotion, exertion, infection, or injury. If an experimenter took the blood pressure of human subjects every week for a year or more he would become conscious of its variation at different seasons of the year and under various environmental influences.

With the appearance of a cold air mass the human body goes through the normal effort of insulating itself, since it is hairless. The peripheral tissues, particularly the skin, respond with a constriction of their blood vessel bed, so that there will be less radiation of heat.

During this stage the body gets a stop signal, so to speak. The body cells in general are less permeable and offer greater resistance. Under these conditions blood pressure shows a tendency to increase. Blood sugar increases because of a greater release from the liver and lessened use in the peripheral regions of the body. A reactive phase follows, and the original trend is reversed. The blood pressure falls.

If a double environmental impact now occurs—for instance, an injury, an emotional upset, or a similar factor associated with the presence of a cold air mass—the body may reveal blood pressure extremes, either high or low. At the crests or troughs we may expect the appearance of sickness.

A change in mood may be another accompaniment. Elation may occur with periods of high pressure and depression with low. If organs in the body are operating in the marginal zone of oxygen and nutrition safety, such wide swings of the blood pressure mechanism may bring defects which are present into the clinical foreground.

If tissue areas exist in the body that are out of step because they have constant difficulty in performing their functions, they too will register distress when the oxygen balance or the water balance can no longer keep pace with the changes that have occurred in the body as a whole, as a result of the necessity to adjust to environmental changes.

During July and August the weather in Vermont is about as stable as it ever gets. As a result the chemical and physiological pendulum swing is fairly normal, with no special strain on the body mechanisms. But let an occasional drop in summer temperature occur, and the pendulum is markedly disturbed in its swing. Blood pressures which have been low will show a tendency to rise sharply.

The reaction of the skin's vast area when it is subjected to cold involves an exaggerated reaction of all chemical, nervous, and hormone factors of adjustment. The result is like a trigger mechanism releasing an explosive force, with results far beyond what might be expected from the seemingly minor environmental alterations.

These midsummer and autumn weather changes in Vermont, although they appear insignificant in themselves, may initiate exaggerated chemical and physiological responses in the body. If there are organs functioning with insufficient reserve capacity then the individual may note the appearance of symptoms indicating all is not well with him.

While these environmental factors play an important part in influencing the swing of the pendulum, much depends on the stability of the nervous system. In part this is determined by heredity, and partially by the conditions prevailing at the time of conception. Obviously it is this variability in environmental factors, with repeated episodes, which ultimately causes trouble in our intricate human machine and brings about the final breakdown we call death.

Variability in environment produced by the annual average of twenty-three storm areas as they pass over Vermont increases the energy requirement for the normal maintenance of the human machine. Every driver of a car is aware of the fact that if he drives continuously at a reasonable rate of speed along a country highway the use of energy in the form of gasoline is far less than when he drives in heavy city traffic and the car must be stopped and started several times within the same block. The human machine is no different in this respect.

Some individuals travel a bumpy biological road. Their poorly adjusted body may show defects much sooner than the same body running on the smooth road of a more stable environment. For those unfortunate people who travel the bumpy road, interfering frequently with the normal biological swing, there are inevitably more blowouts, more knocks, burned-out bearings, and sticky brake bands—in a word, disease. Anyone who travels this road and survives is staunch, enduring, and capable.

We learn from Vermont folk medicine how to control the pendulum's swing by the use of apple cider vinegar; honey; Lugol's solution of iodine; kelp tablets; honeycomb cappings; and a high, natural carbohydrate-low protein daily food intake. With these aids the individual is better able to live each passing day and meet its needs.

Chapter Fifteen

Our Changing External Environment

WE ARE BORN with an elaborate equipment for living. In many respects this equipment is fixed; a baby will never have more than two eyes and one nose. But in many other respects considerable leeway exists at birth for the modification of this constitutional equipment.

The equipment the infant brings with it at birth has been determined in important ways by the hereditary, physical, chemical, endocrine, and nervous impulses to which it has already been subjected. Its further development and health are affected at every turn by its own reaction to different factors in its environment.

Human beings, we may assume, have never succeeded in establishing a way of living in which adaptation to environment has not been a problem that must be solved. This assumption is implied in the stock phrases of the biologist: "the struggle for existence" and "the survival of the fittest."

There are so many factors involved in adaptation to environment that a perfect individual adjustment is perhaps beyond human attainment. All we can hope for is to secure as nearly as possible a satisfactory working adjustment to environment that will allow each individual to live every day with some degree of pleasure and profit.

We do not live in a static world, as everyone knows. Our environment is constantly changing, with increasing speed as the decades of this century go by. Horse-and-buggy days now seem to us in the distant past, and long hours of laborious handwork have given way to mechanical gadgets which make living easier both within and without the home. Vacuum cleaners have replaced brooms. Automatic washing machines do the weekly wash better and quicker than old-

fashioned tub and washboard. Electric and gas stoves eliminate the backbreaking work of making ready a woodpile for
the winter months. Thermostatically controlled oil furnaces
banish coal and ashes. Radio and television provide armchair
entertainment.

It is becoming increasingly apparent that we live in a period of unusually rapid changes in every field—economic,
political, social, and scientific. The tempo of living has
speeded up correspondingly, making increased demands on
the individual. We are faced with the need of a daily
adaptation, both mental and physical, to an environment of
ever-increasing complexity.

Today a baby is born into an environment that bears little
resemblance to the one that molded the bodies and minds of
our ancestors for centuries. Yet the change has taken place
almost without our noticing it or realizing its importance.
Any modification in environment, however, inevitably and
profoundly disturbs all living beings. We have come a long
way since the horse-and-buggy days, when we traveled
slowly but safely along dusty roads, enjoying the scenery
with the assurance that the horse would take us home.

Our manner of living has changed, too, simultaneously
with the change in environment. Each of us does a great
many more things than his parents and grandparents ever
did. We take part in many more events, and every day we
come in contact with more people. Quiet, unemployed mo-
ments are exceptional during the day.

In this modern environment of ours the demands on the
physical side of our make-up have changed. It is a common
observation how little it is necessary for us to walk these
days, even when the distance is short. A good many people
use their automobiles to ride only a few blocks, and jet
planes whisk us over long distances in fantastically brief periods of time. Such body exercise, familiar to countless generations, as walking and running, tilling the land, and manual
labor in rain, sun, wind, cold, and heat, all these have
diminished greatly and in fact have virtually disappeared
among our great urban populations.

These profound changes have occurred within a relatively
short time span, and so it becomes necessary now to evaluate
just how much the substitution of a new mode of existence
for the old one influences the chemistry and physiology of
the human body.

Every living thing depends intimately on its surroundings

and adapts itself to any modification of these surroundings by an appropriate change. The problem, then, is to determine in what manner we have been influenced by the mode of life, the customs, the daily food intake, and the education imposed on us by our present civilization. We must, of necessity, gain a much better understanding of ourselves by doing so, and learn how better to adapt ourselves to our present environment.

The human body is a complex structure made up of many independent cells. In order to bring the whole to any degree of efficiency it is necessary to correlate the action of these cells. That is accomplished by means of hereditary control, chemical changes, endocrine gland secretion, nerve impulses, and our daily food intake.

The body lives in an ever-changing environment which permits rest, work, and acts of defense. These three states make different demands on the factors that correlate cell action. Acts of defense—closing the eyelids at the approach of dust, drawing the hand away from fire, the contraction of muscles for escape from danger—depend upon rapid and correlated action.

At present the environmental load our bodies carry includes food, water supply, weather changes, respiratory hazards, prolonged mental work, insufficient sleep, emotional unrest, unproductive worry, menstruation, accident, industrial injury, micro-organisms, viruses, insects, parasites, drugs, and allergens which produce an allergic reaction.

Health is a state of body and mind resulting from the successful adjustment of the body to environmental factors. Sickness is a departure from health, and is essentially the body's failure to adjust itself satisfactorily to environmental factors.

Between health and sickness there is a presickness zone in which the individual realizes that all is not well. In this zone the body is failing to maintain a satisfactory adjustment to environment, and if that adjustment is not made, because the individual no longer knows how to make it, then he must adjust or be destroyed, in accordance with nature's law. For destructive purposes nature possesses harmful micro-organisms, viruses, and such degenerative diseases as heart ailments and cancer.

As a necessary consequence of failure to adjust there must be an overcoming of the natural elasticity of the body functions beyond the margin of safety. That margin can be illustrated by the buffers of the blood, which keep the blood reaction stable within narrow limits during the course of normal physiological functions.

When the limits of natural elasticity of body functions have been passed, however, changes of a more or less permanent nature will come about, which will be hidden temporarily by a compensatory mechanism permitting the body to function, seemingly without flaw, perhaps, but nevertheless with a certain loss of elasticity. This process may well be continuous, so that in time even the margin of compensation is reached, and for the first time symptoms will show themselves. The margin of safety may be lessened from the very beginning of life by the racial, family, chemical, and anatomical patterns the individual inherits.

The ease with which the body carries the environmental load can be determined by observing the ease with which it recovers from fatigue. Recovery may be rapid, slow, or impossible because of chronic fatigue.

When the environmental load becomes too great to be carried successfully the individual becomes conscious of it by changes in his normal state of well-being that tell him something is wrong. At that point there may be no symptoms present which even a thoroughly competent physician could recognize. But if the situation continues unchecked, in time the symptoms appear which any doctor will recognize readily. That is the beginning of disease.

A business or professional man regards his work as indispensable to the success of his life, and recoils from anything he feels might take him away from it. In the pursuit of his career he regards it as possibly fatal to everything he has worked for if he must take time out to regain his health. For him the path is foreordained—an apprenticeship during which his executive ability ripens, and then a fulfillment of his talents at a time when he has still enough of life remaining to enjoy his reward. If he is to remain undefeated, however, he must be taught how to be sure of his health so he may practice the virtue of endurance. That means he must learn how to adjust himself to his environment, and be able to carry the environmental load successfully.

As I have pointed out, every human body has fighting equipment that enables it to organize for aggressive action, either mental or physical. This organization was intended to be temporary, but our modern environment has made it permanent. When the body organizes for aggressive action, nervous, chemical, and endocrine gland changes take place temporarily, but if the organization becomes permanent the changes are no longer desirable.

Whatever environment an individual finds himself in determines how the body must organize itself. If he lives close to the soil the demands will naturally be primarily on his muscles, and, conversely, if he is in business or a profession his brain will be called upon most.

According to the Bible God created man in His own image—a perfect being. After the creation he was placed in a garden where fruits, berries, edible leaves and roots, and honey were provided as his food. These were all acid in reaction and rich in minerals. The body that was designed for these primitive conditions has been subjected to the pressures of an utterly different environment in our time, but it contains within it still the ability to adjust itself if we would only follow the original plan for daily food intake.

If man fails to consume the needed acids and minerals or processes his food so it is lacking in these elements he becomes sick eventually. He is maladjusted.

Nature has established a wisely directed order for the benefit of man and beast, but in his ignorance man tries to rearrange things. Wild animals, who know better, follow the order and never try to rearrange it. We have to learn that we can live scientifically, yet in doing so follow nature's order.

But let us see what else happens to us in the modern environment which is so far from natural law. When, for example, the sympathetic division of the autonomic nervous system is organized to arouse the body for aggressive action other changes take place in the body. The sympathetic division controls the alkalinity of the blood, so that when it is activated, naturally there is an increase of alkalinity. We can see that process reflected in the change of the normal acid reaction of the urine to alkaline.

Then, as we have already discovered, since calcium is precipitated in an alkaline medium, increased blood alkalinity produces a calcium effect on the walls of the body cells so that permeability of the cell wall decreases, preventing food material and oxygen from entering. The decrease shuts down the cell factory, which manufactures heat, energy, carbonic acid, lactic acid, phosphoric and sulphuric acid. Thus the action of the sympathetic division of the autonomic nervous system and of the adrenal glands cuts off the vital activity of the body cells.

In modern life new factors have appeared in our environment which convert this emergency arousal of the sympathetic division and the adrenal glands into a permanent organization which it was never intended to be. These are the factors:

1. Wheat foods and wheat cereals.
2. White sugar.
3. Pasteurized milk, which changes the normal acid reaction as it comes from a healthy cow to an alkaline reaction not intended by nature.
4. Muscle meats like beef, lamb, and pork, which modern refrigeration has made available for food every day.
5. Citrus fruits and their juices transported to places where they do not grow naturally.
6. Mild or severe cold.
7. Prolonged physical work.
8. Prolonged mental work, made possible by artificial lighting.
9. Emotional upsets.
10. Grief.
11. Unproductive worry caused by the necessity to meet economic needs.
12. Financial upsets.
13. Social conflicts.
14. Family maladjustments.
15. Nervous tension states.
16. Cigarette smoking.
17. Weather changes.
18. Drinking water rich in calcium.
19. Processed foods.

The permanent emergency organization produced by these factors, singly or in various combinations, causes a marked change in an individual's character. Irritability, failure to correlate decision and action, inability to engage in swift action, chronic fatigue—these are some of the symptoms.

Further, the nature of his food intake begins to change. He develops a sweet tooth to supply the liver with the sugar which an overactive sympathetic division demands must be thrown into the blood stream to suffuse the blood. There is a decrease in the desire for vegetables, fruits and natural acid drinks made from fruits, and vegetable juices, with the result that the environmental factors nature depended on to terminate the emergency action of the sympathetic division and adrenal glands are no longer available to the body.

With that failure the permanent organization is firmly established and makes its presence known by the following symptoms:

1. There is a loss of the will to win.
2. Loss of physical and mental endurance takes place.
3. Irritability appears, and the individual becomes unsocial.
4. The face is unusually pale, suggesting the possible presence of anemia.
5. Sensitivity to cold.
6. Feet, hands, and nose are usually cold.
7. There may be increased frequency of urination.
8. The nose is inclined to be wet at times, and there may be an increased amount of moisture in the eyes.
9. Postnasal dripping is generally present.
10. There may be seepage from the paranasal sinuses.
11. Belching of gas from the stomach and heartburn are often present.
12. Digestion is weakened.
13. Constipation is the rule.
14. The systolic blood pressure is likely to be increased.
15. A dry skin is the rule.
16. There is a tendency to thickened places on the skin, as shown by the presence of corns and calluses on the feet.

An individual with a permanent organization of the emergency mechanism in the body may not have all these changes present, but a majority of them will be.

If you want to know whether your body is permanently organized for emergency ask yourself these questions:

1. Do you sleep well at night? Whether your emergency equipment's overactivity is temporary or permanent, sleep will not come when you want it. You will not fall asleep easily, and when you do it will not be sound, and will not bring you to the beginning of a new day refreshed as you would be by normal sleep.
2. Is your appetite good? One of the results of overactivity is a depression of digestive activities, and with this goes a lessening or failure of appetite.
3. Are you constipated? Normal movement of the intestinal tract is slowed when emergency equipment is dominant.
4. Have you gained weight recently? In the emergency state your waistline measurement is likely to increase as time passes.

If you answer yes to these questions there is certainly a temporary or permanent organization of the emergency equipment in the body. It can be terminated by taking two teaspoonfuls of apple cider vinegar and two teaspoonfuls of honey in a glass of water at each meal. One must, in brief, know how to restore the body physiology and chemistry to normal. I have learned how to do this from Vermont folk medicine. I have summarized the prescription, but let me spell it out a little more carefully now.

Besides the vinegar-and-honey treatment, we must return to natural foods. White flour foods and white sugar must be removed from the daily food intake because they are highly refined, which removes the minerals the body depends on to rebuild and maintain body tissues. Without these needed minerals the body deteriorates, like a piece of land that has lost its fertility and run down.

A man's inheritance may carry him to fifty years of age, but after that it is up to him to rebuild his body and maintain it successfully during the later years if he wishes to come to the sunset years with good eyesight, good hearing, mental and physical vigor, and no appearance of senility.

Native Vermonters living close to the soil refer to white flour, white sugar, packaged cereals, and processed foods as "civilized foods." They exchange white flour bread for rye or corn bread and other rye and corn foods. Corn oil is used in cooking. This oil helps allergic conditions.

I learned from Vermont folk medicine that a child with asthma who wheezes at bedtime will stop and get a good night's sleep if he gets a tablespoonful of corn oil. In an adult it decreases the wheezing fifty per cent if taken at bedtime. Corn oil, furthermore, if applied to the eyelids at bedtime as one applies an ointment to the edge of the eyelids, will favorably influence granulation.

For these and other reasons corn oil is used in cooking because it contains several unsaturated fatty acids which help to terminate the organization of the emergency organizing equipment.

White sugar is exchanged for honey to sweeten foods, because it acts as a sedative and has a mild laxative action. Muscle meats like beef, lamb, and pork are taken only once a week because they stimulate the emergency equipment. Meat is exchanged for eggs, cheese, fish and other seafood. Yogurt and cottage cheese are also valuable foods to help terminate the emergency situation. Citrus fruits and their juices must be removed from the daily intake if you live in the northern part of the United States.

Heat changes the chemistry of the body, which is shown by the presence of an alkaline urine reaction before taking a hot bath and the presence of an acid reaction afterward. In Vermont, cold produces an alkaline urine reaction and citrus fruits produce the same thing in the majority of natives. For that reason we exchange citrus fruits and their juices for fruits that are grown in cold climates, like apples, grapes, and cranberries. All these grow wild in Vermont.

As I study the foods native Vermonters remove from their intake I have learned that the majority of these foods shift the normal acid urine reaction to alkaline, which is evidence that they activate the emergency organizing equipment. Instead of them the Vermonters use leafy and root vegetables, berries, apples, grapes and cranberries, honey, nuts, fish, game, and poultry.

To these may be added a food supplement in the form of kelp tablets. I learned about the use of kelp from Professor Cavanaugh, of Cornell, who did a great deal of research on it. Because of its mineral and vitamin content derived from the ocean it represents an ideal food supplement.

The potassium in honey, kelp, apple cider vinegar, vegetables, fruits and berries will depress an overactive emergency organizing equipment and lessen its activity so that it will be available only when needed. Two teaspoonfuls of apple cider vinegar and two of honey in a glass of water, taken at each meal or between meals, will also help a great deal to bring about this happy and healthy result.

Chapter Sixteen

The Weather

I AM INDEBTED to a friend from Chicago, the late Dr. William F. Petersen, for teaching me the relationship between a human being and the weather. Dr. Petersen had read some medical articles of mine and invited me to be a guest at his home, where we could talk about the work he had done in relating weather conditions to the state of the human body.

I accepted the invitation eagerly. Vermont has what may well be the most unstable weather pattern in the world, and I was anxious to learn everything I could about its influence on my patients. During the three days I spent in Dr. Petersen's home he gave me an intensive course in the work he had done, and I followed this up with a study of his books on the patient and the weather, which he gave me. Later we had further conferences and exchanged letters, in which I gave him my own observations of Vermont weather and its effects.

Everyone who has arthritis is acutely conscious of the relation of weather to his disease. I believe it will help the arthritic patient, and others as well, to understand what happens in the human body when the weather changes.

Three factors make up climate: variations of temperature, of humidity, and of storms. The zone of greatest variation in temperature is not in the tropics or in the Arctic, as one might suppose, but in the temperate zone. The variations there, where most of us Americans live, are so great that the body has to be especially equipped to handle them. Thus, in the winter, our internal heating plant is stepped up in order to keep us warm. Seventy-five per cent of the daily food intake is used for this purpose.

When the outdoor thermometer goes down under the onslaught of a cold wave the blood becomes more alkaline. All physiological processes in the body are altered; the energy expending mechanism increases its activity and the human motor shifts into high gear. These changes mean more pain for the victim of arthritis, and he is likely to take more aspirin to lessen his discomfort. Since aspirin is an acid, it combats the increased alkalinity of the blood caused by the temperature drop. Another way to do it is by taking at each meal two teaspoonfuls of apple cider vinegar and two of honey in a glass of water.

If the need to relieve pain is very great the amount of vinegar and honey may be increased by adding two tablespoonfuls of each to a drinking glass, then stirring with a spoon until they are well mixed. Fill the glass with water and stir again until the whole of the contents are thoroughly mixed. Because heat lessens the alkalinity of the blood an electric heating pad will also help to lessen pain.

Until a cold wave has passed and there is a rise in the temperature reading it is helpful to make changes in the daily food intake. Your bread should be either rye or corn bread. Honey should be used instead of white sugar because it is acid in reaction. Citrus fruits and their juices should be avoided because they produce, at least in the majority of individuals who live in the northern part of the United States, an alkaline urine reaction which reflects an increased blood alkalinity.

Muscle meats like beef, lamb, and pork also increase alkalinity, as is demonstrated easily by the urine test with nitrazine paper I described earlier. A high protein diet—milk, eggs, cheese, meat, fish, and poultry—is another cause of an alkaline increase. Eat, instead, a low protein-high natural carbohydrate diet of the kind provided by nature—fruit, berries, edible leaves and roots. Yogurt is acid in reaction, as is cottage cheese. These two often work well together in shifting the urine reaction from alkaline to the normal acid reaction. Cranberry juice and sauce are two other acid aids that may be tried by the arthritis sufferer to lessen blood alkalinity and combat the effects of a cold wave.

If he is confronted by the painful discomforts of a cold wave the person with arthritis should try to remember what is happening in his body and realize that simple treatment measures will help to lessen his pain. It is a simple pattern, this increased blood alkalinity resulting from a temperature drop, which changes the chemistry of the body tissues and alters all the physiologic processes.

The remedy, then, can be summarized with equal brevity: aspirin, vinegar and honey at meals, the use of heat in some form, and an adjustment of the food intake. All this will shift his motor to low gear and keep it there.

An arthritic patient with a barometer in his home is able to note, by following the readings from day to day, that pain appears or increases on a falling barometer and decreases or disappears when the pressure rises. By keeping a careful watch he will be able to institute the treatment I have described when the barometer begins to fall, and thus avoid much or all of the pain associated with a cold wave. When the pressure begins to rise again he may lessen the treatment if he desires.

We have much still to learn about the relationships between weather and human health. What I have described is only a single facet of a complex subject, but I believe the lesson it contains will be of considerable help to arthritis sufferers.

Chapter Seventeen

Biologic Food Selection

THE ARTHRITIS VICTIM is usually more than ordinarily interested in what he eats. He wants to know what foods he should consume to speed recovery, or whether there are some that may hinder him. I have made a considerable study of the whole subject of food selection, and in this chapter and the one following I will report in more detail than before on what I have learned.

It has been assumed by many writers on diet that a daily food intake could be devised that would be perfect for any human being. The prescription is simple, they say. Take the ideal number of calories, the ideal amount of protein, fat, carbohydrates, minerals, and vitamins as well. Then add the psychological adjuncts of flavor and variety. Given this balance, so the argument goes, it would be possible to produce, from the nutritional standpoint at least, a prize-winning human. And that, as far as I am able to estimate, is the doctrine of the ideal standard diet.

But can we prove this in the laboratory? Normal white rats, for example, may be measured by weight, degree of development, type of behavior, character of coat, and capacity for reproduction, and one could raise a group of these little animals on a standard ideal diet. It is also obvious, even to the untrained observer, that there is a difference between differently nourished white rats under perfectly controlled experimental conditions.

Yet, when I talk to my farmer friends I discover that prize-winning farm animals cannot be created so easily. They are brought to a high standard by giving them the foodstuffs which are directed most nearly to the individuality of the animal. Farmers tell me that in preparing animals for state or county fair exhibits they must pay attention to the individual needs of the stock to be exhibited.

Some animals, for instance, drink more water than others. Some eat more salt. Some must be given food easily digested, which means delicate food. In their natural environment, close to nature, cattle and horses eat cafeteria style. Each one selects here and there the food required to satisfy its own individual needs.

A study of racial and family patterns shows that humans should not be fed alike either, if our purpose is to put them in the best state of health. Nowhere, it seems, should greater homage be paid to individuality than in the matter of what is eaten. Yet textbooks and articles on the subject persist in talking about a "normal diet." But there is no such commodity in the sense that there is any diet which will make for a maintenance of normality.

There is, of course, an average, customary "will do" diet. It is an habitual ingestion of foods which enable the individual to go along his usual way without becoming obviously starved, undernourished, or ill.

It has been contended that the normal person, left to his own devices, will select the food best suited to his own peculiarities and the demands of his body. This is only partly true, however. Infants, permitted to choose for themselves, pick the foods that make them grow better than those fed on the strictest, supervised regimen. Animals, too, if allowed to select, will take the foods they need.

As for man, he was given instincts by nature to guide him in food selection, and those instincts guide him during childhood in the choice of his food, but as I have noted, he leaves them behind when he becomes an adult. His taste, like his sense of his own needs, is perverted early in life. Few adults are able to trust their own ideas of what they should eat.

One of the most common manifestations of disturbance in body nutrition is the tendency to put on weight as the individual grows older. He stops growing at both ends of his body, but he is likely to continue growing in the middle. This represents unoxidized food material which has not been properly burned in the body.

In the final analysis all food must be prepared for us by animals, plants, bushes, or trees, else we cannot assimilate it. As we grow older we digest more slowly, our appetite is less, our stomach and digestive juices are no longer as vigorous. They have lost the vigor that carried away everything coming in contact with them, and have become sluggish.

At this time of life the native Vermonter appreciates his two teaspoonfuls of honey and two of apple cider vinegar in a glass of water, because he has learned that its use at mealtime improves his digestive ability and contributes to his feeling of well being during the day.

It is not mere entry of food into his stomach, intestines, and blood that is important, but what happens to it after it gets there. In the body there is a sort of biochemical brew in which a number of reactions are going on at the same time. We can so select our food that we interfere markedly with these reactions, or we can choose in such a way that they are assisted.

Because the average person is so far removed from the soil it is extremely difficult for him to know what foods he should select for his daily intake. He knows that the seasons of the year bring different foods for his consideration, and what remains of his childhood instincts tell him that it is desirable to eat these foods in season. But he seems to have forgotten that nature knows more about diet than man, and that he will find in the fields, woods, lakes, or ocean, in whatever part of the world he lives, the food best suited to his needs as long as he lives there.

He must also remember, however, that he is a member of a race, and the experience of that race during past centuries has determined what his racial diet should be. No matter where he lives ultimately he must necessarily follow his racial diet as far as possible, if he is to enjoy his best health. There has been transmitted to him a type of body that works best on the kind of food determined by the race to which he belongs.

By means of the food intake nature seeks to maintain a working balance between the two divisions of the autonomic nervous sytem. Food grown in cold climates seeks to calm down an overactive sympathetic division. Food grown in warmer climates seeks to stimulate this division. Consequently we should be reluctant to eat food imported from a climate different from the one we live in, unless it is a food common to one's racial diet.

If the end result of the daily food intake is to secure and maintain a working balance between the nervous, endocrine, and chemical mechanisms that organize the body for aggressive action, mental or physical, and those that organize it for peace and quiet, how is the average person to know what his daily food intake ought to be so that the desired result will be attained? How can he secure this working balance, meanwhile maintaining mental and physical efficiency and avoiding the appearance of sickness? What yardsticks can

he use to estimate for himself whether his food meets his
body needs from day to day as the seasons change?

The yardsticks do exist. One of the first he can use is the
urine reaction taken in the morning with nitrazine paper,
which I have described earlier. An acid reaction, you will
remember, suggests that the osmotic pressure of your blood,
which regulates the passage of fluids through membranes in
the body, is as it should be, and that the amount of hydrochloric acid normally secreted by your stomach when food
is taken is adequate for your needs. It suggests, too, that the
sympathetic division is under control and the body motor
is in low gear. The parasympathetic division, which builds
and stores reserves, will be in the driver's seat. You should
be feeling well, and equal to the day's demands.

Remember, however, that if you take your urine reaction
within three hours after eating food it will normally always
be alkaline, because of the alkaline tide in the body which
accompanies eating.

When you have an acid urine reaction on rising in the
morning you can eat protein foods, like beans, peas, milk,
eggs, cheese, meat, fish, or poultry during the day. But if
you recall, there is an old nutritional law, formulated during
the days when bloodletting was a form of medical treatment in Vermont, that says you must take an acid when protein food is eaten in order to avoid, or at least lessen, its
thickening influence on the blood.

That can be done, of course, by mixing a glass of the familiar vinegar-honey-and-water solution and sipping it during the meal, as you would a cup of coffee. You can also
take it before breakfast or during the morning if you wish.
A little experimenting will enable you to decide which time
is best for you.

As you take it try to remember that you are drinking the
mixture to thin your blood so it will not be thickened by
protein food eaten for breakfast. You want your blood to
pass easily through the tiny blood vessels in the lungs, liver,
and other organs of the body. You don't want an increase
in your blood pressure resulting from a molasses kind of
blood trying to circulate in your body. You do want your
brain to have an adequate supply of blood so that during
the day you will have the ability to think clearly and make
decisions promptly.

But let us consider now what happens if your urine reaction in the morning turns the nitrazine paper blue, indicat-

ing the unwanted alkaline reaction. This will suggest that your blood is thicker than it should be and doesn't easily pass through the capillaries, consequently it will upset the blood timetable.

Normally the blood makes a complete circuit every twenty-three seconds, but now it will take longer. Instead of being faintly alkaline in reaction it is hyperalkaline. A dairy cow's milk that changes to alkaline also becomes thick, like soup, and flakes soon appear in it which join together to form lumps. As we have seen, vinegar poured over the ration brings about a reversal: the lumps disappear, then the flakes, until finally the milk is normal.

There is no reason to believe that the behavior of alkaline reaction milk and of alkaline human blood are any different. In humans the liquid part of the blood does not pass easily through the sievelike walls of the capillaries, as ink passes through blotting paper, and so the blood pressure is higher.

You are likely to have some dizziness when your morning urine reaction is alkaline. The amount of hydrochloric acid normally secreted by your stomach may be less than normal. You may have heartburn and gas formation in your stomach after eating. The energy expending mechanism is still active, but there is very little gas in your tank, or none at all. You awake feeling tired, and face the day without the will to win.

With such a reaction the indication is to eat none or at least very little, protein food during the day. Instead, live out of the garden and orchard. If protein is taken it should be only a little, and preferably from the ocean. Eat fruit for breakfast, but be sure it grows in the climate of your part of the world. You can also eat a vegetable soup with herbs, in dehydrated form, sprinkled over it. These herbs are ordinarily available in grocery stores in small glass bottles. Take a teaspoonful of chopped dehydrated parsley either directly from the spoon or mixed with your food.

If you eat a dairy product let it be yogurt, which is acid in reaction. Cottage cheese, remember, is also acid. Swallow one kelp tablet at each meal during the day, because it represents a vegetable grown in the ocean. It contains minerals, vitamins, and amino acids that supply body needs. Remember that the composition of the human body and seven gallons of sea water equal one another.

At every meal take the vinegar-honey-and-water solution, sipping it while you eat, and at the same time take at least two extra teaspoonfuls of honey, using it to sweeten the food or taken directly from the spoon. If comb honey is available eat this at the end of the meal, and chew the honeycomb cud that appears in the mouth until it disappears.

During the middle of the morning and the middle of the afternoon take the vinegar-honey-and-water treatment again. In my opinion it is the greatest of all pick-up drinks. It will change the nervous, endocrine, and chemical mechanisms of your body back to normal. It will thin your thickened blood and establish a normal osmotic pressure. It will lower your blood pressure.

To take your urine reaction in the morning when you rise and then use the result as a guide to your food intake during the day is only a substitute for the instincts nature gave you, and that you left behind long ago when you grew up.

As another guide to your food selection you should examine your urine in the way I have learned from native Vermonters. Urine is passed in a glass, so that it may be held up to the light and studied. Normal urine should be amber in color. If it is dark it suggests that too much salt is being ingested, either through the salt shaker or from salty food. Check your salt intake to see if this is true.

A light colored urine, on the other hand, may represent no more than dilution by an increased water consumption. But it may also be produced by an increased intake of foods containing potassium, like fruit, berries, and edible leaves and roots.

By noting whether the urine is dark or light in color one gets a working knowledge of the sodium-potassium balance in the body, and indicates the need of increasing or decreasing the intake of salt or fruits, berries, leaves and roots.

If the urine is cloudy it is usually alkaline in reaction. Cloudy urine, again, suggests too much protein in the diet but in order to determine whether that is the reason add a teaspoonful of apple cider vinegar to the urine in the glass. If the cloudiness clears up only partially add a second teaspoonful. If the cloudiness then disappears, it indicates an excess of protein, and the amount of vinegar required to clear up the urine indicates roughly the amount of protein intake.

Should excess be the case, you must lessen your protein consumption until it is reduced to the point where the urine is no longer cloudy. You will also want to take the vinegar-honey-and-water dose at mealtimes, to increase your acid consumption. Remember, always, the old law: An acid must be taken when protein food is served.

Chapter Eighteen

What Vermonters Eat

IN OUR STUDY of biologic food selection let us take another look at those native Vermonters who have always lived close to the soil and see what foods they select, guided by those childhood instincts which they have never lost.

I have spent a great deal of time discussing with aged Vermonters what it is they eat which brings them to the later years of life with good eyesight, good hearing, and mental and physical vigor with no evidences of senility. As I have said, they tell me repeatedly to stay away from "civilized foods." They mean, of course, the white flour foods, white sugar, packaged cereals, and processed foods for which they have substituted rye or corn flour, honey instead of white sugar, and natural rather than processed foods.

They told me, these old Vermonters, that natural foods gave them the strength to do farm work—strength they could not get from packaged cereals and other processed foods. Repeatedly they advised me to eat as little as possible of foods that come out of a factory.

I was told, too, that I must maintain a proper balance between natural carbohydrate foods and proteins. The daily food intake provided by nature is high natural carbohydrate and low protein. If you rearrange this natural selection by eating a low carbohydrate-high protein diet you may expect the appearance of sickness from time to time.

The natives also called my attention to foods made from wheat and wheat cereals. Vermonters advised me to stay away from them. When I asked why, they told me that these foods lessened the ability to do farm work. On the other hand, they said, foods made from corn lessen fatigue and increase endurance.

If a scratch feed containing wheat is thrown down for hens to eat, they will leave the wheat and eat the remainder. They will only eat the wheat if they are hungry later and there is nothing else for them. I asked what happened when they did eat it, and learned they would lay soft-shelled eggs which might not hatch, and if they did, the chickens would be weak.

In place of wheat foods native Vermonters advise foods made from corn, like corn bread, corn-meal mush, and popcorn. They found still another reason for eating foods made from corn instead of wheat, by watching how cows like to get into the cornfield, and how they refuse to eat a ration containing much wheat. Hens, too, like cracked corn.

In the majority of Vermonters wheat foods produce an alkaline urine reaction and so it is only logical to remove them from the diet, with rye and corn foods substituted. Eliminating wheat foods means removal from the daily intake of any food made from white flour, whole wheat, graham, or buckwheat flour, in addition to wheat cereals and such other foods as cake, crackers, cookies, and doughnuts.

Besides wheat and wheat cereals, I was advised to avoid white sugar, which should be exchanged for honey. One of the twelve adults who served as human guinea pigs while I was trying to learn whether sickness appeared on an alkaline or acid urine reaction background told me that she had discovered one reason why her reaction shifted to alkaline from time to time. It happened, she said, whenever she ate candy, which occurred every time her bridge club met.

I reported this observation, in turn, to the others in the control group who were keeping daily reaction records and food diaries, and asked them to watch and see if the same thing happened when they ate candy. It was true, they told me later. From these reports and the finding that sickness appeared on an alkaline urine reaction I concluded that the native Vermonters were right when they said that white sugar should be exchanged for honey.

The third food my Vermont friends warned me against was milk as a beverage. Here, to check what I had been told, I enlisted the aid of a dozen small children under five in addition to the twelve adults who were keeping careful records for me. Both these groups were keeping a daily food diary and urine reaction record.

On the theory that little children are guided by natural instincts my small guinea pigs were allowed to select what they wished from food placed on the table. Much to my surprise, they would not drink milk. That was a shock to me, because in prescribing a nutritional program for a patient I always used milk as an anchor and built the rest of the prescription around it. These children, by their refusal, told me I was wrong.

What they wanted and liked very much were sour drinks.

Their favorite was cranberry juice. When it was made from cranberries in the home they wanted it so sour that adults in the family would not take it.

But I was curious as to why these children would not drink milk when they had a free choice. I engaged a farm girl to take a milk reaction with nitrazine paper at the afternoon milking of each cow in a herd of forty-five registered dairy cows, and under the supervision of the herd owner she did so. Every week she gave me a written report, and from it I learned that milk as it comes from a healthy cow is weakly acid in reaction. Then I studied the reaction of pasturizing, which is necessary to make milk safe for human consumption. Under pasteurizing, I found, milk changed from acid to alkaline.

There was my answer. Because pasteurized milk was alkaline the children who were guided by their instincts refused to drink it, and these same instincts led them to seek sour acid drinks.

Two mothers who were in the habit of taking their children on picnics in the summer did an experiment for me. On one occasion they took three different drinks for the children. One was the "hayfield drink," used in Vermont for a good many years, which was simply our old friends vinegar and honey added to every glass of water used in making whatever quantity was needed. The second drink was lemonade, and the third was milk. The children were told they could have any of the three, and all of them chose the vinegar-and-honey drink. After it was gone, they turned to the lemonade, drank that up, and would not touch the milk.

A fourth food producing an alkaline reaction which my aged Vermont friends had either restricted or eliminated from their diets was muscle meat—beef, lamb, and pork. You may well ask what they do with the farm animals they slaughter, and the answer is that the meat goes to market as part of the farmer's income, but he usually saves for his family the liver, heart, tongue, stomach, sweetbread, and kidneys. A portion of the liver is often given to neighbors, knowing that they will return the favor when they have an animal ready for market. This custom of saving the internal organs for home use has been handed down from one generation of Vermont farmers to another, and is still observed.

But even with what relatively little they save of this muscle meat, the farmers are cautious. They limit their beef, lamb, and pork to one serving a week, and they eat lamb the least,

because it is the quickest to produce an alkaline urine reaction. Instead, they eat fish and other seafood as a source
of protein, knowing that it is much less likely to be alkaline.

Native Vermonters also told me to keep away from citrus
fruits and their juices, especially oranges and grapefruit.
When I asked why, they told me that these fruits produced
stuffy ears, what they called "the orange-juice cold," an itch-
ing skin, and rough red places on the skin that looked as
though they had been rubbed with a rough towel. They also,
it was said, increased the pain in arthritis and produced painful joints.

When Vermonters go to Florida during the winter, however, they can eat oranges and grapefruit without suffering
any of the ill effects that occur when they eat these fruits in
Vermont. Apparently, if one lives where oranges grow, they
serve as food, but if they are imported to a colder climate the
body will not accept them.

Apples, grapes, plums, and bush cranberries grow wild in
Vermont, which shows that nature believes malic acid in
apples; tartaric acid in grapes; and malic, quinic, and benzoic
acids in cranberries are best for those living in a northern
climate.

Let me summarize here what I have learned from native
Vermonters about the daily food intake which will avoid an
unwanted alkaline urine reaction, with consequent illness:

1. Eliminate from your diet all sweets like pie, cake,
   candy, ice cream, pastries, soft drinks, and sweet des-
   serts of every variety. When it is possible use honey on
   all the foods you want to sweeten. It is both a sedative
   and a mild laxative, and promotes sound sleep at night.
   It contains everything the body needs. The honeybee
   probably knows all there is to know about nutrition.
2. As far as it is possible eliminate white flour, which
   means avoiding white bread, cake, waffles, pancakes,
   cookies, crackers, and doughnuts. Bread should be rye,
   corn, soybean, or pumpernickel. In Vermont popcorn is
   often used instead of bread.
3. Eliminate all cereals except oatmeal, corn flakes, corn-
   meal mush, etc., with cream or milk. Sweeten with
   honey. Use milk in cooking, not as a beverage. There is,
   for example, a cereal prepared for market which contain oats and maple syrup, with no added salt.
4. Eat two vegetable salads and one egg every day.

5. Eat meat once a week, and liver one or more times. Liverwurst may be used instead of liver. Eat fish and seafood often. Heart, kidney, sweetbread, tripe, and tongue may be taken frequently, and fowl occasionally.

6. Eat apples, grapes, apple sauce, cranberry sauce, grape jelly, or apple jelly once daily.

7. Drink grape, apple, cranberry, tomato, or V-8 juice every day.

8. Do not eat oranges, grapefruit, or pineapple, or drink their juices, if you live in the northern part of the United States.

9. Suitable starches may be taken: potato, rice, pumpkin, cornstarch, bananas.

10. Suitable sugars may also be taken: honey, molasses, maple syrup, maple sugar, raisins, figs, and dates.

11. These are suitable proteins: all game, fish, clams, crabs, shrimp, oysters, cheese, eggs, and nuts.

12. Suitable fruits: all berries, apples, apricots, cherries, currants, grapes, peaches, pears, plums, and prunes.

13. Suitable vegetables: artichokes, asparagus, fresh green beans, beets, beet tops, brussels sprouts, cabbage, carrots, cauliflower, celery, corn on the cob, cucumber, dandelions, endive, garlic, green peas, kale, leek, lettuce, olives, onions, oyster plant, parsley, parsnips, peppers, radishes, sauerkraut, spinach, string beans, summer squash, tomatoes, turnip, watercress, and all leafy vegetables.

14. Suitable fats: bacon fat, butter, cod liver oil, cream, lard, corn oil, olive oil, and peanut oil.

The biologic food selection I have described in this chapter and the one preceding is best for those with arthritis. It is really just a new name for the diet of our forefathers, which is many centuries old. It removes from the daily food intake all those foods that produce an alkaline urine reaction in the majority of individuals. It is a diet composed of essentially the same materials, although possibly in different form, as those our ancestors ate. In them it produced strong, sturdy people, and it is suited as well for us now as it was for them.

Modern civilized diets differ from the biologic food selection principally by the introduction of refined foods. With the elimination of these foods the instincts which guided our forefathers in food selecting once more take charge, and without fail they guide us to the biologic food selection I have described, if it is available. We must always remember that our environment has changed but our bodies are the same as they were a thousand or ten thousand years ago, as far as chemical function is concerned.

Arthritis victims who follow biologic food selection may expect to see the efficiency of their body chemistry increase gradually, and as this occurs, the arthritis will gradually disappear.

One must keep in mind, however, that there is a great difference in the ability of people to respond to a change in nutrition. Ability does not depend so much on age as it does on how long the individual and his immediate ancestors have been the victims of faulty nutrition. If, for example, your father's and grandfather's family were from Europe or the British Isles, where conditions on the whole have been better than in the United States for that ancestry, the response to a change in nutrition is usually prompt. But if your immediate predecessors were Americans, the response is less prompt. If several generations of Americans precede an individual the response is likely to be slow.

In general, chemical reactions both inside and outside the body are regulated in two ways. First, they depend on the nature and quantity of the substances involved. Second, the speed of their reactions can be made to vary. Two substances may react together for a long time, but so slowly that no apparent change has taken place in them. Such a chemical reaction, which in itself proceeds with the utmost slowness, may be speeded up under certain circumstances by adding the mere trace of a third substance known as a catalyst. This outsider, the catalyst, acts as a stimulant of the reaction.

It is hard to conceive of a living organism maintaining its existence for a moment without the help of catalysts. Most of the chemical changes that constitute digestion, the use of food by body cells, and the excretion of waste would take place far too slowly without them. Not enough energy would be supplied in a given time to keep the cells of the body going.

For catalysts in our nutrition we turn to the trace minerals found in fruits, berries, edible leaves, edible roots, and honey. One or two teaspoonfuls of honey taken at every meal will provide the catalysts needed to speed up the handling of food by the body.

Anyone who cares to examine the biologic food selection for vitamin and mineral content will find it adequate for both. As I have said, the object of this selection is to remove only the foods which produce an alkaline urine reaction in most individuals. It also represents an effort to return the individual to a high natural carbohydrate-low protein diet, which is what nature has provided.

The value of any diet is determined by its influence on the urine reaction. People who develop sickness on an alkaline urine reaction recover when the reaction becomes acid and continues that way. Biologic food selection aids greatly in maintaining an acid urine reaction, and consequently it is a primary aid in the maintenance of continued good health.

After biologic food selection had been worked out in Vermont it was tried by members of a correspondence study group that I organized, and they continued it for a period of twenty years. This group represented thirty-two different states and the Hawaiian Islands. Most of its members were nationally known. In the two decades they practiced this selection—and that is certainly an adequate experimental period—they got the same results that native Vermonters had been getting for two centuries. The practice should bring the same results to you.

Chapter Nineteen

How to Check Your Body Performance

VERMONT FOLK MEDICINE has developed several ways in which someone with arthritis can check his body performance. It would be helpful for an arthritic patient to do this every week so that he could learn whether his human machine was working in a normal way and following nature's plan.

You can learn a great deal about your body machine and how to manage it by studying the number of times a minute you breathe when you're seated in a chair. Bring a mirror close to your mouth and breathe on it. A film of moisture will be deposited. Now take a rubber bulb, like the one on an atomizer, squeeze it and blow air on the mirror. There will be no moisture film.

This experiment tells you that the air you breathe out is different from the air you breathe in. Expelled air has more water, as the mirror test shows, but what you can't see is that it also contains carbonic acid. The number of times you breathe each minute will tell you whether your body is trying to get rid of moisture and acid, or whether it is trying to keep both inside.

To visualize this and other processes it is helpful to remember that the human body is a machine for the production of energy. In a heat machine or a combustion machine—and that, of course, is what the body is—oxygen from the air around you is absolutely necessary. When you breathe air into your lungs you bring oxygen against a very thin membrane which separates the air in the lungs from the blood in the capillaries, which permit the blood to pass through the lungs. The oxygen in the air passes through this membrane to enter the blood, which carries it to the body cells.

The active part of the blood carrying the oxygen is the red blood cells; the portion of the red blood cell which does this job is a chemical compound called hemoglobin, and the unit of hemoglobin which unites with the oxygen is its iron content. Iron has an affinity for oxygen.

The red blood cells, with their hemoglobin loaded with oxygen, finally reach the body cells. There the oxygen, along with food materials also carried by the blood, is transferred to every cell that needs oxygen, in order to burn the food material and produce body energy.

As a result of the vital activity of body cells waste material accumulates which is transferred to the red blood cells that have unloaded their oxygen. The cells carry this material back to the right side of the heart, and from there it goes to the lungs to be unloaded and take on another supply of oxygen.

The amount of oxygen needed by the body varies from time to time. For example, muscular exercise obviously calls for more than when you sit quietly in a chair. These varying needs are adjusted by the rate and depth of the breathing movements. The regulation is wholly automatic, being governed by a breathing center at the base of the brain. If a needle should be thrust into this center and manipulated so that the nerve cells are destroyed, breathing movements would cease and death occur.

What keeps the center sending out regular messages to

the breathing muscles? What makes it slow these movements when the need of the body cells for oxygen is satisfied?

Here is the answer. The accumulation of carbonic acid in the blood stimulates the breathing center and causes it to send messages to the breathing muscles to make the breathing more rapid. If you hold your breath the carbonic acid begins to accumulate in the blood immediately. The blood passes through the center, and as the carbonic acid accumulates, a point is reached where the center sends messages to the muscles to breathe and you find it necessary to start breathing. No voluntary effort on your part can prevent it.

While you are at rest, seated in a chair, count the number of times you breathe during one minute, or have someone count them for you. The normal number will fluctuate between sixteen inhalations and sixteen exhalations per minute to eighteen inhalations and the same number of exhalations, for a normal adult. It has been established that the figure of sixteen is the normal count for a healthy adult.

Do you breathe more or less than the normal? It will be helpful for you to learn the answer, because if you are breathing less than the normal your body is trying to keep within it the carbonic acid that the body cells make. It needs acid and is doing the best it can to keep what it makes. Your slower rate tells you that you should increase your acid intake.

The Swedish and Norwegians answer this need for acid by drinking coffee, which is acid in reaction. The English supply it by drinking tea, also acid. Others get it by taking alcoholic beverages like beer, wine, or liquor, all of them acid.

In Vermont the need is best supplied by the vinegar-and-honey treatment. Used instead of coffee in the morning, tea in the afternoon, or drinks at the cocktail hour, it represents an excellent building food which shifts the human motor from high gear to low. It enables you to relax, and later helps in producing sound, refreshing sleep. It is a drink that contains the healthful qualities of apples, preserved in the vinegar, and the equally healthful attributes of nectar from flowers in the honey. Both contain minerals and vitamins needed in maintaining and rebuilding the body.

If your breathing is less than the normal sixteen times a minute you should avoid wheat foods, wheat cereals, white sugar, muscle meats, and citrus fruits, because all of these, as we have seen, increase the alkalinity of the blood, and that slows the breathing rate in order to hold carbonic acid in the blood stream.

Fruits, berries, edible leaves, edible roots, and honey are indicated as food because they are all acid in reaction before they enter your mouth. Their addition to the daily food intake will help you at once if you have a slower than normal breathing rate. You should follow through then with the kind of biologic food selection we discussed in the previous chapter: rye or corn bread; fish and seafood instead of muscle meat; apples, grapes, and other cold country fruits instead of oranges and grapefruits, provided you live in the northern part of America.

Besides your breathing rate, the pulse beat in your wrist will tell you much about your human machine and how to manage it. The arteries contract and expand with the contraction and expansion of the heart, and these processes constitute the pulse which can be felt in the larger arteries located near the surface of the body. The pulse rate per minute is usually in direct proportion to the temperature of the body, running from the normal rate of 72 beats per minute in an adult, to as high as 130 to 140 when a fever is present in sickness.

A pulse rate slower than the normal indicates that food material is being brought to each body cell at a slower rate than normal. It also indicates that when this material enters the cell it is being burned at a slower rate than it should be, suggesting that the material does not pass easily through the cell walls. A lessened permeability of these walls may be making the passage more difficult.

A slow rate also suggests that potassium is lacking in the daily food intake. Potassium is needed to increase the permeability of cell walls, and to keep the flame in each cell burning brightly. There may be a lack of the associated minerals which serve as little matches to start that flame, so food material can burn and acids needed by the body to carry out physiological processes will be liberated. Potassium is a magnet for fluids, and its lack tends to dry out and shrink the body cells, which naturally interferes with their work.

As I studied Vermont folk medicine I found that it was helpful for me to think of each body cell as containing a small candle with the ability to burn even though surrounded by the cell's watery content—in short, like a candle burning under water. I always try to determine, when I treat a patient, how this candle is burning. Is it feeble or is it burning too fast?

Another way to learn something about your body is by studying your temperature when it is taken by mouth. As everybody knows, the normal is 98.6 degrees. Everybody ought to find out whether his normal temperature is always 98.6, or whether it is always below that figure, because the knowledge will be useful in illness.

But there is more to the business of temperature than readily appears. Remember, first, that through conduction, radiation, and evaporation heat is constantly lost from the body. This loss is counterbalanced by the liberation of heat within you resulting from the burning of food within the body cells.

In warm-blooded animals this adjustment under normal conditions is accurate and even. When heat is produced rapidly, as in violent exercise, the loss by evaporation through lungs and skin prevents more than a slight elevation of body temperature.

Every cell in the body is a producer of heat. It gets the material to produce heat from the food taken in, and whatever heat is produced is delivered to the body's various parts. When you are exposed to heat or cold, however, a pronounced change occurs in the mechanism that presides over body temperature. In fever the temperature rises not because of the extraordinary production of heat, but because the normal regulating mechanism has been changed. A body temperature below normal tells us there is a lessened activity of body cells as a whole.

During every twenty-four hours your temperature rises and falls at certain times of the day and night as metabolism speeds up and slows down. When your temperature is high you are wide awake and full of pep. When it is low you are sleepy and listless.

There are three main kinds of temperature cycles. If you are the kind of person who pops out of bed in the morning, sings his way through a brisk shower, and shows up at the office full of energy you belong to the morning group. Your temperature when you awaken is higher than it will be about three or four o'clock in the afternoon. If you place a thermometer under your tongue at 10 A.M. and again at noon, before eating, you will find that the latter reading marks the peak of your temperature and energy. After lunch there will be a slow decline.

The evening group experiences just the reverse. If you belong to it, getting out of bed is painful, facing breakfast
an ordeal, and lasting through the morning a daily struggle.
But about two o'clock your temperature will start to rise,
and by late afternoon you will be as sharp as the morning
group was at 10 A.M.

The third group comprises people who seem to be perky
in the morning, suffer a decline about noon, endure a dull
afternoon, and come back to life during the evening.

To find out which group claims you, take your temperature when you awaken and every three hours after that for
the remainder of your waking period. Follow the usual pre-
caution—that is, don't take it immediately after drinking hot
or cold liquids, always wet your lips, and close them tightly
around the thermometer for three minutes.

If you record these readings every day for not less than a
week, preferably two, you will be able to tell at what time of
day you reach your energy peaks. If your highest temperature occurs regularly in the period before 1 P.M. then you
belong to the morning group. If it occurs from 1 P.M.
to midnight you are in the evening group. Temperature
rises both in the morning and late evening show that you are a
member of the mixed group.

The general belief that a temperature above 98.6 degrees
always means sickness is wrong. Everyone has small daily
temperature fluctuations. Some people fluctuate as much as
three degrees during the day, though most of us do not vary
more than one degree. Children have a wide range. For
adults the normal temperature can be anywhere from 96.7
to 99.

What can you gain by going to all this trouble? Generally
speaking, you can make improvements in your daily life by
taking advantage of your energy highs, because performance
and resistance to fatigue vary directly with the temperature.
It is helpful to people with arthritis if they understand this
fact, and all of us can use the knowledge in these ways:

1. On your job you can often do your most important work
    during your best period by skillfully arranging your time.
2. At home you can perform your most difficult tasks at the
    apex of the daily curve.

If necessary, you can raise your low body temperature by
taking a hot bath, and in doing so increase your ability to
do work or to get more enjoyment from a social event

scheduled to take place at a time when your temperature is at its low point.

Turning now to another aspect of self-examination in the interests of health, you should learn to study the color of the gums of your upper and lower front teeth. Normally they should be pink, but as you examine them from day to day in time you will be able to recognize quickly any change in their color. They will either show an increased redness or they will be paler than the normal pink. The redness indicates that you have a high phosphorus content in your blood and a low level of calcium. Similarly, paleness is a sign of low phosphorus and high calcium. Normal pinkness can be taken to mean that phosphorus and calcium are in balance.

Study the tongue side of the lower front teeth and note whether tartar is deposited there. If so it indicates that calcium is not being held in solution, and you need to take an acid like apple juice or apple cider vinegar every day to hold the calcium and prevent further deposits.

You can tell a good deal about the way the cells of your body are burning the food that comes to them by studying the color of your gums. The increased redness mentioned above indicates they are burning it faster. It indicates, too, that your basal metabolism has increased, and that you are a self-starter with plenty of energy to do the day's work, with your human motor in high gear, but you find it difficult to relax when the quiet moment comes at the end of the day. If, however, you take the Vermont folk medicine remedy, vinegar-honey-and-water before or during the evening meal, you will be able to shift into low and get some rest. Nature will reward you by organizing your body for peace and quiet.

When the color of the gums of your lower front teeth is pale your body cells are burning food slowly. The basal metabolism is lower. You are no longer a self-starter, and you lack energy. Probably you have cold hands and cold feet. Your motor is in low gear, and you are likely to be tired all the time—morning, noon, and night. In short, you are suffering from chronic fatigue.

Such a condition simply means that you have lost your knowledge of nature's plan, or have never heard of it. That is the time to examine your daily food intake and begin the biologic selection process, avoiding the civilized foods and substituting for them the natural foods which will give your body the acids and minerals nature intended it to have. At breakfast take a glass of apple juice, some grape juice at lunchtime, and cranberry juice at the evening meal. You can, of course, arrange these three juices in any other order you wish. If the food budget does not permit buying them, add one or two teaspoonfuls of apple cider vinegar to a glass of water and sip it during meals.

Still another self-examination is to test the reaction of the skin on the inside of your forearm with nitrazine paper. First allow water from the cold water faucet to run into a small glass and test its reaction with the nitrazine paper to find out whether it is neutral in reaction, as it should be, to make the test. The paper should not change color if the water is neutral.

Then wind a small amount of absorbent cotton on one end of a toothpick, making a cotton wound applicator. Dip the applicator in the water and apply it to the inside of the forearm. Usually three applications will make a wet place large enough to receive a strip of nitrazine paper.

Now place the strip on the prepared wet spot and pat it into place with the unwound end of the toothpick. Allow it to remain in place until all the paper is wet, then remove the strip and examine it for the reaction. If the skin is acid in reaction, as it is normally, the paper will turn yellow, but if it is alkaline the color will be a shade of blue.

The yellow reaction indicates that your skin is eliminating acid from your body as it should, but the blue shows that the body cells may not be manufacturing acid properly, or else it is being held within the body because the blood is too alkaline and needs the acid to use up the buffering ability of the blood's sodium bicarbonate content.

If the test shows that your skin is alkaline you need the vinegar-honey-and-water treatment at each meal. You also need to take an apple cider vinegar sponge bath at least once a day. Simply add a teaspoonful of vinegar to a glass of warm water, place the stopper in the washbowl, and pour in the contents of the glass. The solution is then applied to the skin surface with your hands, with a cloth wrung out of it, or best of all with a sponge. Don't wipe your skin with a towel but let it air dry, which it will do very quickly. The skin takes up apple cider vinegar rapidly.

There are still other methods of checking the way in which your human machine is working. I have described earlier the method of determining whether your urine reaction is alkaline or acid, and how to shift it to the acid side if it is alkaline.

You can also gather a great deal of helpful knowledge if you study the reaction of your food before it enters your mouth. Nature has spread acid about with a lavish hand in fruits, berries, edible leaves and roots. During the warmer months of the year a Vermont farmer will eat the leaves of forty-five different plants and bushes, and eight different trees.

I know a scoutmaster who is teaching the boys in his troop about survival rations, showing them how to gather food from the fields. He began by instructing them how to prepare milkweed greens, using the smaller leaves of the plant. Next he taught them to utilize certain ferns which resemble the curled top of a violin where the pegs are inserted—commonly called fiddlehead ferns. Prepared as food, these ferns are delicious and taste like asparagus.

In time the scoutmaster hopes to take his troop out on a hike carrying no food with them, and be able to gather what they need from the fields, which offer an abundance of acid reaction foods, as survival rations.

While you are studying food remember that boiling water makes it alkaline. Native Vermonters are in the habit of adding vinegar to water in which food is to be cooked, so that the food may retain its original acid reaction. At the table vinegar is used on every food possible. Thus they observe nature's law—that food must be acid in reaction before it enters the mouth.

For your own information you can test food reaction before you eat it with the aid of nitrazine paper. Then, with the help of knowledge gained from studying your urine reaction, you should carry on a little research and learn what foods produce in your body the unwanted alkaline urine reaction and remove them from your diet. Similarly, you should learn what foods produce the normal acid reaction and eat them.

Every individual, bear in mind, is a law unto himself in this respect. You have had transmitted to you a body that works best on foods which produce the normal acid reaction and is hampered by those which bring about the alkaline reaction. Everyone needs to work out his own daily intake by studying the influence of foods on his urine. What may be right for you may be all wrong for somebody else, even in your own family.

You should remember that there are other factors besides food which produce an alkaline urine reaction. I have mentioned some of them before, but here they are again: mild

or severe cold, prolonged physical or mental work, emotional
upsets, grief, unproductive worry, financial upsets, social conflicts, family maladjustments, nervous tension states, cigarette
smoking, and weather changes. All these have to be taken
into consideration in evaluating the reaction of your urine.
But their mere presence, singly or in combination, would
indicate the need of taking vinegar, honey, and water at
each meal.

Now let us summarize what we have learned about checking on the performance of the body. Here, in brief, are the
self-examinations we can all make:

1. Testing the reaction of the skin on the inside of the forearm.
2. Taking the body temperature, pulse, and breathing rates
   per minute.
3. Studying the color of the gums.
4. Paying attention to the daily food intake.
5. Checking the amount of work and play, the hours of
   sleep, and the state of the emotions.
6. Watching adaptation to weather changes.
7. Checking the temperature of the air breathed during the
   day and during the night.
8. Determining whether you are tired all the time and lack
   endurance to do the day's work.

From all of these examinations we can gain a knowledge
of how the tiny candle in each body cell is burning. If it
burns as it should it will create heat to keep the body warm.
There will be no cold hands or feet, and there will be abun-
dant energy for work. The cell will manufacture carbonic
acid, lactic acid, phosphoric acid, and sulphuric acid as it
normally should so that the breathing rate per minute does
not have to slow down to keep acid in your body.

By rearranging the daily food intake, by taking the vinegar-honey-and-water treatment at every meal, by trying to
balance work and play, and by learning how to ride out the
storms of life—by all these means the tiny candle is regulated
so that it burns more nearly as nature intended it should.

Honey taken every day is the body cell's best friend. It
contains what every cell needs. The honeybee has carefully
selected everything that goes into the formation of honey,
and it is a magnet for fluid. It stops the tendency of the cell
to dry out, and makes it take in fluid so that it swells again

to its normal size. It brings to each cell the minerals that ignite the candle flame anew, and provides the kind of sugar it can burn.

For the person who has a breathing rate below sixteen per minute or a pulse rate below 72, honey every day is a necessity, because it creates within the body the new supply of energy needed to do the day's work. It brings freedom from mental and physical fatigue, and it is a sedative that promotes sound and refreshing sleep. I shall always be grateful to Vermont folk medicine for teaching me all these things about honey.

When you make the quick checkup of your health from day to day that I have advocated in this chapter there are four questions you should ask yourself. They are:

1. Do you sleep well at night?
2. Is your appetite good?
3. Are you troubled by constipation?
4. Have you recently gained weight?

If you can answer yes to the first two questions and no to the last two you can give yourself a clean bill of health. But nevertheless make a progress report for yourself from week to week or month to month so that you can determine whether improvement is taking place in your body performance. If it is and you are an arthritic patient the chances are that your arthritis will show an improvement too.

Chapter Twenty

Questions Asked about Apple Cider Vinegar

I GET a good many letters asking whether apple cider vinegar thins the blood, dries it up, or produces anemia. It always amazes me that some people are so greatly concerned about the dire results that may follow from the vinegar-and-water treatment, when they think nothing of dousing a leafy salad with vinegar and never dream of an untoward result.

I also get letters asking me to recommend an apple cider vinegar that is suitable for medicinal use. There are several such good vinegars on the market. Unfortunately there are also some made from apple peelings and cores after the pulp has been used for some commerical purpose, and these are not suitable for medicinal use. The kind I recommend should be made from the whole apple, because apple pulp contains what is medicinally useful. I customarily look at the price of the vinegar, knowing that the kind made from peelings and cores is sold at a much lower price.

When you decide on an apple cider vinegar to be taken from day to day, choose one that has a pleasant taste and is accepted by your stomach. If your stomach rebels at two teaspoonfuls in a glass of water, without the honey added, then reduce the amount to a teaspoonful. If even that much is unacceptable try another brand. Vinegar whose label reads "full strength" usually has a good taste and is well accepted by the stomach.

If you are not getting the medicinal results you should get from taking it try another vinegar. An excellent brand made from unsprayed wild apples and unpasteurized before it is bottled is made by the Saltmarsh Cider Mill, at New Boston, New Hamsphire. Some full strength vinegars I know about are Sterling Cider Vinegar, made by the Sterling Cider Company of Sterling, Massachusetts, and Musselman's Apple Cider Vinegar, made by the C.H. Musselman Company of Biglerville, Pennsylvania. If a natural foods store or a health store is available I feel sure you will find in stock a full strength vinegar suitable for medicinal use.

The standard mixture I have advocated in this book, which is the centuries-old Vermont drink, is two teaspoonfuls of vinegar and two of honey to a glass. Stir until well mixed, then fill the glass with water. You can add the two teaspoonfuls of honey to a glass of apple juice, if you wish.

I have heard it said that acid harms the body, but if an acid derived from fruit like the apple is harmful why has nature spread acid about with such a lavish hand in fruits, berries, edible leaves and roots? I have offered vinegar mixed with drinking water or ration to chickens, hens, minks, cats, dogs, goats, dairy cows, calves, bulls, farm horses, and race horses. Always an improvement in health resulted. If vinegar was harmful in any way I would certainly have observed some adverse reactions.

My wife and I have taken vinegar and water every day for thirty years, as nearly as I can remember. Most of the time we have added the two teaspoonfuls of honey. The results have been excellent in every way. For example, as conductor of the Barre Junior Symphony Orchestra for twenty-two years, I have missed only one weekly rehearsal and never missed a concert, which shows what the treatment did for me. My daughter has taken vinegar for eighteen years. The three of us, as a family, are resistant to disease, free from colds, and rarely ill.

DOES APPLE CIDER VINEGAR THIN THE BLOOD?

For those who are concerned about whether vinegar thins the blood, I would call their attention to the observation made during the days when bloodletting was a form of medical treatment in Vermont. It was noted that protein foods thickened the blood and vinegar thinned it. As a result of this observation the nutritional law I have mentioned before came into being: an acid to be served with protein food in order to lessen the thickening influence of protein on the blood.

Today vinegar is poured over baked beans. Cranberry sauce, containing four different acids, is served with fowl. A slice of lemon is served with fish and other seafood in a restaurant. Apple sauce, containing malic acid, is served with pork and ham. Mushrooms, containing citric acid, are often served with steak. All these acids served with protein foods are designed to lessen the thickening influence of protein.

But we fail to observe the old nutritional law when bacon, eggs and pasteurized milk are the foods, and we often do not take an acid when other protein foods are eaten. As the blood thickens, due to this failure, it does not pass as easily and quickly through the capillaries in the lungs, liver, and other body organs, with the result, as we have seen, that the blood timetable is upset and the cells do not get their food material as promptly as they need it. More pressure is required to push the thickened blood through the capillaries, and so there may well be an accompanying elevation of blood pressure.

It is truly a vicious circle, but it can easily be broken with the vinegar-and-honey mixture at every meal. If high blood pressure, for example, comes from the consumption of too much protein and too little acid taken with it, vinegar alone in a glass of water will drop the pressure from twenty to forty points in a half hour. The vinegar-and-honey mixture also contributes to a feeling of greater well being because the thinner blood circulates quickly and more easily through the capillaries.

To answer the question, then, we should not be worried about vinegar thinning the blood, but rather direct our concern to the thickening influence of protein food when an acid is not taken with it.

DOES APPLE CIDER VINEGAR DRY UP THE BLOOD?

On the contrary, it safeguards the body from loss of blood. If a dairy cow passes blood with her bowel movement, four ounces of vinegar and the same amount of water given by mouth from a bottle morning and evening every day will soon stop the condition. If blood appears in the milk, the treatment is equally certain. Similarly, if blood appears in the urine of a dog, a teaspoonful of vinegar added to his ration once a day, if he is a small dog, or a tablespoonful if he is a large one, will cause the condition to disappear in three weeks.

Bleeding hemorrhoids also yield to the taking of two teaspoonfuls of vinegar in a glass of water at every meal. A man taking that treatment will observe, too, that if he happens to cut himself while shaving there will be very little bleeding.

If a child bleeds frequently from the nose and no injury is present, a teaspoonful of vinegar in a glass of water three times a day, with or without meals, will soon bring about a cessation. An adult troubled in the same way needs to increase the dose to two teaspoonfuls.

A woman who is still menstruating can reduce the amount of her menstrual blood about fifty per cent by taking this same vinegar-and-water treatment at every meal, and the number of clots will be greatly decreased as well. If the menstruation is profuse every month the vinegar will reduce it to normal, or nealy so.

Patients facing surgery who are given one or two teaspoonfuls of vinegar in water at each meal or between meals for as long as possible before the operation will have only a small loss of blood at surgery, and postoperative hemorrhaging rarely occurs in them. Sometimes there is an oozing of blood following an operation, and this too can be stopped with a teaspoonful of vinegar in a glass of water every half hour. Vinegar and water three times a day after an operation will shorten healing time and speed the patient's recovery.

I spent considerable time trying to discover why vinegar influences body bleeding, and learned finally that bleeding takes place on an alkaline urine reaction background. Later I leaned that the tendency to bleed stops when the urine reaction is changed from the alkaline to the normal acid. From these two observations it became evident that bleeding was related to body chemistry, and a hyperalkalinity was associated with a tendency to bleed. Changing the blood to a hypoalkaline state by taking vinegar diminished or stopped entirely the bleeding tendency.

By noting the bleeding time when a cut is made on your body you can get some idea of your own blood reaction. If it is too alkaline the bleeding time will be prolonged, but if it is not the time will be short. If the cut bleeds longer than it should and is hard to stop you need the vinegar-and-water treatment one to three times a day, to change your body chemistry. Test your urine reaction, in the manner I have described, and continue taking the vinegar until you have a normally acid urine reaction. Test the urine one or two days every week for a time to see whether it has changed back to alkaline.

No, I say to my questioner once more, apple cider vinegar does not dry up the blood. Indeed, it prevents loss of blood from the body, and it is this very quality which has led people to think that a drying up occurs. It keeps blood within the body to nourish the cells better. The blood is such a vital fluid that the body will make every effort to keep it.

You influence your body chemistry by means of the food you eat, the liquid you drink, and the air you breathe. Ask yourself: Are you living out of the garden, the orchard, and the ocean as you should, or are you living on civilized foods? The answer to this question is the answer to your state of health.

DOES APPLE CIDER VINEGAR CAUSE ANEMIA?

Anemia is a medical term meaning a lack of red blood cells or a lack of the proper amount of hemoglobin they ordinarily carry.

You manufacture red blood cells in the marrow of your bones. About three per cent of these cells is destroyed every day, and they must be renewed. To renew them you must take into your body daily all that is needed to make normal blood cells, and to make enough of them. If you fail in this task because of improper eating there will not be enough normal blood cells to carry oxygen to the body cells. Food intake is an essential element in another aspect of this whole process, for it is the food you eat and the liquid you drink that makes the bone marrow where red blood cells are made.

Physiology textbooks tell us that we make a new blood stream every twenty-eight days. Daily replacement of blood cells that are destroyed and complete cell renewal in twenty-eight days are not the result of luck or accident. If new blood cells are born as fast as old ones die health is maintained, and the body continues to be an efficient human machine. On the other hand, if the new ones are not born as fast as the old ones die the balance is destroyed, and the body begins to show less efficiency as a human machine. Remember that a trillion red blood cells are used up every day and have to be renewed.

Every tissue and organ in your body has to draw its replacement material from your blood stream. Whether it is your eyes, muscles, heart, stomach, liver, or whatever other organ, this is true. Perhaps that will give you an inkling of the tremendous power you possess when you know how to control the quality of your blood by a daily intake of the right kind of food, the right kind of liquid, and the proper kind of air breathed into your lungs.

Most of us become aware at some time or other, often painfully, that we can never be successful—socially, economically, or financially—without good health. Without a knowledge of how to build and rebuild our bodies we cannot hope to dominate life, and it will in fact soon dominate us. Daily living should be a series of absorbing adventures. One who enjoys good health welcomes problems and difficulties, and neither avoids them nor fears them. Nor does he complain about them or admit defeat.

With this basic idea firmly governing what we eat the products of orchard and field, plant and vine will become increasingly important in our lives. Fruits and vegetables are fundamental in perfecting the body and bringing health to its highest point. The growing things of the plant kingdom are filled with prodigious values in the maintenance of health. Trees and plants take up dead metals from the earth and change them into living minerals. According to Vermont folk medicine your body as a whole changes every twelve months, and the medium of body change is the food we eat, most importantly from these sources.

When a dairy cow that has been getting vinegar with her ration is slaughtered for beef it is observed that the bone marrow, when the bones are sawed through, is a healthy red color, while the cow without the vinegar exhibits a pale-colored marrow. The meat of the vinegar-rationed cow is a rich maroon color and the tallow is very white, while those without vinegar have a paler meat color and the tallow is yellow.

The bone marrow of turkeys that have had vinegar added to their drinking water and the marrow of mice that also got vinegar both showed a marked increase in marrow redness.

Turning to human beings, it is true that vinegar and water at each meal increases the amount of hemoglobin in the blood, which means that more red blood cells carrying hemoglobin are present.

It is significant, I think, that organized medicine often prescribes for a patient with pernicious anemia one-half to one teaspoonful of dilute hydrochloric acid in a glass of water at each meal.

Remember, once more, that you control the quality of your blood by a daily intake of the right kind of food, the right kind of liquid, and the right kind of air. Apple cider vinegar helps you to control the quality of your blood, and as I have shown, it definitely does not produce anemia, but has quite the opposite effect.

I might add that when we ask nature if apple cider vinegar causes anemia, the answer is easily found in demonstrating how the health of fowl, animals, and man is improved when vinegar is taken at every feeding.

Chapter Twenty-One

The Treatment of Arthritis

IN THE PAST TWO CENTURIES Vermont folk medicine has come to the conclusion that arthritis can be successfully dealt with only if the patient understands why various treatment measures are used. He must understand the fundamentals of his disease in order to combat it. The individual who has been fortunate enough to escape the ailment also needs this knowledge so that he can avoid it.

Vermont folk medicine believes that failure to understand how arthritis is produced, and how to deal with it if it appears, may result in crippling. It believes that the sooner effective treatment is begun, the better are the opportunities for an individual's normal biochemical processes to bring about recovery. In some people arthritis appears to be a self-limited condition, while in others it is only terminated when suitable treatment is applied.

Most people are aware, in a vague sort of way, that the body is a wonderful mechanism. Both in its construction and its ability to maintain the processes of life the body presents marvels no human ingenuity could ever equal. The precision with which it functions, its equilibrium, and its powers of adjustment have been viewed with deep wonder by scientists of every age.

If not interfered with, these powers are always asserting themselves for the preservation and protection of life. The human body is constantly exposed to changing conditions, and just as constantly demonstrates its ability to adjust itself to these changes. That ability is readily apparent whenever difficulties or obstacles arise.

Arthritis is encountered more often in the city than in the country. The joints that do most of the work are the most subject to disturbance: hands, elbows, shoulders, hips, knees, and feet. Arthritis of the small joints, like those in the fingers, seems to be much more resistant to treatment and more firmly rooted in a deeper underlying cause.

Months are required to cure arthritis—seldom less than three, and sometimes more than eighteen. The longer the disease has persisted the longer it takes to cure, as a rule. Under any form of treatment recovery from chronic arthritis in the majority of individuals is not one of uniform uninterrupted progress, but rather a progress interrupted by temporary setbacks.

In sum, the improvement follows an undulating course, with the periods of improvement gradually lengthening and those of relapse shortening until the symptoms ultimately disappear. It is desirable, even imperative, that the patient understand this to avoid disappointment and prevent discouragement.

Overactivity of an incompletely recovered arthritic joint

always results in a relapse, and this the patient must learn. Underactivity of arthritic joints is preferable to overactivity. As improvement comes, the tendency is to use the joint too much.

The arthritic patient should recognize that even when he is symptom-free he is not a person with normal joints, but one whose joints are reactive to many conditions to which others are insensitive. For the time being he is restricted to a mode of life within his articular limitations, which are decreased only cautiously and gradually as improvement takes place, and he must pursue a way of living as close as possible to his articular tolerance. Ample rest and adequate exercise are necessities obtained by thoughtfulness and self-control.

Vermont folk medicine does not recognize a difference among bursitis, gout, rheumatoid arthritis, osteoarthritis, and muscular rheumatism. In earlier years they were classified as manifestations of the presence of rheumatism in the body, but now they are referred to as arthritis and they are all treated in the same way.

In treating arthritis folk medicine first prescribes two teaspoonfuls of apple cider vinegar and two of honey in a glass of water at each meal, sipped like coffee. The honey may also be added to a glass of apple juice, as a variation. Let us consider the reason for this prescription.

Vermont folk medicine believes that the treatment of arthritis begins in the stomach. We learn that the stomach digestive juice is a thin, light-colored fluid which is acid in reaction. The acidity of this juice, which is made by cells in the lining of the stomach, is due to free hydrochloric acid. The acid secreted by the cells acts as an antiseptic or germicide and prevents putrefaction in the stomach.

When the acid is diminished in quantity or is absent, as it may be, there is no check on the growth of micro-organisms in the stomach. Fermentation may take place, with the formation of large amounts of lactic acid and butyric acid.

How the stomach is able to produce a secretion about three million times more acid than the blood is not known. Vermont folk medicine has learned that two teaspoonfuls of apple cider vinegar in a glass of water taken before eating spoiled food will prevent the appearance of ptomaine poisoning. If this preventive is not taken, a victim of the poisoning can recover in a day if he sips frequently from the vinegar-and-water dose.

This demonstrates the ability of vinegar to act as an antiseptic or germicide to prevent putrefactive processes in the stomach. We already have seen that vinegar, honey, and water during meals will greatly improve digestion and bring about a disappearance of heartburn and gas formation in the stomach after eating.

Under normal circumstances the secretion of gastric juice in the stomach is constant. Even in fasting there is a small, continuous secretion, but during eating and throughout the period of digestion the rate is greatly increased. Secretion is usually started by the sensation of eating, the taste and odor of food. This is supplemented later by chemical actions in the stomach.

Hydrogen combines with the blood chlorides to be secreted on the stomach wall as hydrochloric acid. This acid helps to regulate the opening and closing of the stomach, and enters the small intestine. There it stimulates the production of secretin by the glands in the first part of the small intestine. Secretin acts to increase the flow of pancreatic juice and bile. A lack of normal stomach acidity would tend to reduce the production of these vital secretions.

The digestion of proteins and minerals requires a normal digestive secretion. Calcium metabolism, for example, is highly dependent on the hydrochloric acid content of the stomach, and in its absence only the water soluble calciums are available. The acid soluble mineral salts remain in crystalline form and are not absorbed.

People with arthritis are usually classified as calcium deficient, although they do tend to accumulate calcium deposits. Vermont folk medicine says they are not making hydrochloric acid in the stomach, or else the amount made is too small. Normal calcium metabolism is so highly dependent upon this acid that when there is a lack of it a disturbed calcium metabolism is inevitable.

From all this I am sure you can see how important it is to provide the stomach with a proper amount of acid when food is taken. Otherwise the process of digestion is not carried on in the way nature intended.

In the absence of hydrochloric acid Vermont folk medicine believes that minerals held in solution in fruits, berries, edible leaves and roots by their acid content are no longer held in solution in the stomach. Instead they are precipitated, as they are in the teakettle when acid is lacking.

To prevent precipitation of minerals and return them to solution if precipitated, vinegar and water at mealtimes is the best answer. The lesson Vermonters learn when they remove mineral deposits from their teakettles by adding vinegar and boiling water is simply applied to the stomach.

Let me summarize, then, the various reasons why Vermont folk medicine prescribes apple cider vinegar in arthritis.

Reason One: To provide acid the stomach is supposed to furnish but does not, so that the work this acid does in the stomach may take place. As a result of its study of arthritis folk medicine has arrived at the conclusion that treatment begins in the stomach by providing the acid necessary to carry on an adequate digestion of food taken at a meal. Apple cider vinegar is the natural selection for that purpose.

Reason Two: To make the tissues of the body tender, so that body cells may carry on their vital activity as they should. When these cells improve their activity the tissue juices are improved. The tenderizing of tissues, making them unusually tender with improved tissue juices, is easily demonstrated by pouring a teaspoonful of vinegar down the throat of an aged hen that has been selected for killing. After this dose is repeated morning and night for three days and the hen is killed on the fourth day, her meat will be unusually tender and have a delicious taste. Without the vinegar the meat would be tough and tasteless.

Making body tissues tender with vinegar may also be demonstrated by pouring two ounces of it over a dairy cow's ration twice a day for a week. When she is slaughtered after this treatment her meat will be unusually tender and tasteful. Without the treatment, as in the hen, the meat would be tough and without taste. In fact, vinegar poured over the ration of a ten-year-old cow twice a day will make her heart as tender as that of a two-week-old calf, when it is served on the table.

The second reason, then, that vinegar is prescribed is to make the body tissues tender. When they are tender they maintain their youth, and age very slowly. One of the secrets of aging slowly and avoiding a wrinkled skin is to take vinegar, honey, and water at every meal. In rebuilding the human body vinegar is of great service.

Reason Three: To produce elasticity of tissues in the body. This ability of tissues to stretch easily is observed in dairy cows, goats, and dogs when they give birth to their young. When I first studied the mixed herd of fifty-four dairy cows difficult and prolonged labor among them was common.

Help was often needed in order to bring the calf from the cow. But after adding vinegar to the feed the time required to give birth was fifteen minutes, with no assistance needed. This short period was the result of greater tissue elasticity produced by the vinegar.

Elasticity can be obtained in the human body in the same way. Obviously it will delay aging, and enable a man in his later years to be in good physical condition, able to do farm work if that is his occupation.

Reason Four: To remove calcium deposits in blood vessel walls. A continued study of the bodies of dairy cows after they had been slaughtered showed that a change had taken place in the deposit of calcium generally present in the larger blood vessels. When cutting through the larger blood vessels extra pressure on the knife was required.

But after the addition of vinegar to the ration, extra pressure was no longer needed; these larger vessels cut as easily as any of the other tissues, showing that calcium was not precipitated in the blood stream but held in solution. It was additional evidence that the reaction of the blood permitted calcium deposited in blood vessel walls to enter into solution again. This ability is, of course, a desirable characteristic when arthritis is present.

Reason Five: To promote the use of calcium in the body. As the pouring of vinegar over the ration of dairy cows was continued, it was observed that no undersized calves were born. Instead, they were of normal size, with strong, rugged legs. Goats were also larger when they were born. Chickens grew faster and feathered out more quickly when a half-cup of vinegar was added to every gallon of their drinking water. When a young bull was dehorned, his horns were found to be solid instead of hollow.

By the addition of vinegar to the ration it was possible to add from fifty to a hundred and fifty pounds to the weight of a newly purchased bull or cow. When the animal was slaughtered, the increased weight was found to be present in the bones. They were larger than normal, and there was little porous bone present. The teeth of an older cow looked like those of a much younger one.

With the aid of vinegar, apparently, calcium had been held in solution until it was deposited in the body where it would normally be, rather than in places where it was not intended to be deposited.

The bones are a storehouse for calcium, and the ability to

deposit calcium in the bony framework of the body with the aid of vinegar is certainly of value in elderly people, because it makes the bones stronger and much less likely to be broken.

Reason Six: To terminate activity of the body's energy expending mechanism. This is another valuable service performed by vinegar in the animal and human body. Vermont folk medicine calls it "sweetening the disposition."

As we have seen, when the energy expending mechanism becomes active it organizes the body for aggressive action and puts it on a combat basis. The human motor is shifted into high gear. If this activity is not ended, dogs, horses, and bulls, as well as humans, become irritable and difficult to live with. Dogs, horses, and bulls can be calmed down within one or two months and made easy to handle by the addition of vinegar to the ration. So can humans, by taking vinegar, honey, and water at each meal. "Race horse" children, as I have shown in two examples, can be dealt with by the same method. The secret is simply to shift the human motor from high to low gear.

Reason Seven: To exert a favorable influence on constipation, which is often present in arthritis.

Reason Eight: To improve the health of the skin. It is easy to see how vinegar mixed with food improves the outer covering of animals' bodies. Under this treatment the hair of cats, dogs, horses, and cows will lose any roughness and become smooth, developing an excellent gloss. Fleas will leave the bodies of cats and dogs in one or two months. Cows will lose their lice in about the same period of time. In humans the skin will increase in health and demonstrate it by an improvement in color, a decreased inclination to wrinkle, and freedom from blemishes. Best of all, for most of us, the skin will age slowly.

Reason Nine: To kill the culture medium in the body that makes possible the growth of harmful germs. Vermont folk medicine believes that sickness often makes its appearance because the body has become a suitable culture medium for the growth of harmful germs. The object of treatment is to break up this medium, as one might break up a similar one in the laboratory by adding too much of this or that ingredient. Too much acid, for example, will kill a culture medium, and vinegar is prescribed by folk medicine to kill the medium in which the germs grow. The soil represented by body tissues and fluids is then no longer suitable soil for such growth. It becomes unsuitable by the taking of apple cider vinegar.

Reason Ten: To assist in shifting the blood mass to the digestive and other abdominal organs. Another belief of Vermont folk medicine is that vinegar will assist in shifting the blood mass from the second and top floor vascular bed (which includes the heart, lungs, central nervous system, eyes, ears, the lining of the nose and throat, and the muscles of the arms, legs, and body trunk) to the ground floor vascular bed (which includes the skin, stomach, intestines, liver, spleen, and kidneys).

Reason Eleven: To bring about the disappearance of putrefaction in the intestional tract. The odor of the bowel movement is due to skatole and indole, two substances formed in the course of putrefactive processes occurring within the intestine. If two teaspoonfuls of vinegar in a glass of water are taken at each meal the bowel odor will disappear in a month or two, showing that the putrefactive process in the intestine no longer takes place.

These eleven reasons for drinking vinegar and water at meals provide ample evidence of how Vermont folk medicine has learned by trial and error to prescribe vinegar for many of the ills of the human body, including arthritis.

Let us consider, then, why two teaspoonfuls of honey are added to the vinegar-and-water solution when it comes to the specific treatment of arthritis.

Reason One: Honey improves digestion; it is the stomach's best friend, as the old Vermont saying goes. Native Vermonters have told me repeatedly that honey is very soothing to the stomach. Acid in reaction, it helps to provide the acid the stomach needs to carry on its part in the digestion of food.

Reason Two: It has the ability to attract fluid—commonly referred to as its hydration ability. This is due to the potassium honey contains, and to a sugar called levulose, which has more moisture attracting ability than any other sugar. You can see this quality for yourself if you bake bread or pastries. Both remain moist and palatable for an indefinite period. You can observe it, too, when you eat salty food. If honey is taken with salty food there will be much less desire for water.

Reason Three: It helps the body to destroy harmful germs. A serious study of Vermont folk medicine involves a consideration of how the body cells take in and give out fluid—that is, hydration and dehydration. Folk medicine believes that bacteria needing moisture to maintain themselves get it by taking it from the body cells. But if there is enough potassium in each body cell, it will draw moisture from the bacteria instead of the reverse.

The constant contest between bacteria and body cells, therefore, determines whether the cell's attraction for water is strong enough to take it from the bacteria, or whether the moisture attracting ability of the bacteria is strong enough to withdraw moisture from the body cells.

By taking care to eat foods which are a source of potassium —fruit, berries, edible leaves and roots, and honey—the body cells are provided with the moisture attracting potassium needed to win the contest with bacteria.

The arthritic patient who takes the vinegar-honey-and-water treatment with every meal is in a better position to win this contest with any bacteria that may be present.

Native Vermonters teach the younger generation the drawing ability of honey by putting a red apple in a small glass jar and adding enough honey to fill it. As it floats in the jar the apple will be almost covered with honey.

The cover is then put on the jar, and at the end of a week the skin of the apple will be wrinkled, showing that it is too large for the apple pulp. By the end of three weeks the red color of the skin will have left the apple and be present in the honey, while the sweet apple taste will be gone. When the apple is eaten it will be tasteless and lacking in moisture.

By this demonstration a young Vermonter is taught that if he takes honey at each meal the movement of fluid in his body will be influenced favorably by the honey's moisture attracting ability. The nutritional value of foods will also be improved by the ability of honey to extract from them what the body needs.

Reason Four: It is an excellent food supplement because it contains vitamins, minerals, and enzymes. If an arthritic patient wants to be doubly sure that his daily food intake is adequate for his body's needs he should take two teaspoonfuls of honey at every meal, by itself or added to a glass of vinegar and water. There is everything in honey that seems desirable from a nutritional point of view.

To begin with it contains vitamin B_1, called thiamine; vitamin B_2, riboflavin; and vitamin C, ascorbic acid. To complete the list it also contains pantothenic acid, pyridoxine, and nicotinic acid.

The minerals in honey are even more important than the vitamins. They comprise potassium, sodium, calcium, magnesium, iron, copper, chlorine, manganese, sulphur, and silica. As these minute quantities of minerals, essential for bodily health, are used up in certain body processes they need to be replaced constantly. Eating honey is the simplest means of getting them into the body.

We need to remember that honey also contains enzymes, as they are called. These enzymes are present in the digestive juices, consequently they aid digestion. Yet honey itself requires no process of digestion before it can be utilized by the body. Nor can micro-organisms affect it adversely, for if they come into contact with it they are quickly destroyed.

In short, honey is a perfect food from a medical point of view. It contains no harmful chemicals, and not more than one hundredth part of it is waste. It is truly the ideal food supplement to fill any gaps that may be present in the nutrition of an arthritic individual. It is taken at every meal to insure continued good health.

Honey is not just another sweet. It is really a medicinal sweet that will help greatly in maintaining the body's health. The human body works on a minimum of what it requires; honey contains that minimum.

Reason Five: It has a laxative effect, which aids in preventing constipation. The effect comes from its levulose content. This is a sugar which is slowly absorbed and eventually reaches the large intestine. Honey is a laxative, but a mild one.

Reason Six: Honey is a sedative to the body. It produces sound, refreshing sleep by shifting the human motor from high to low gear.

Reason Seven: Honey helps to relieve pain in arthritis. It also helps to bring about a disappearance of muscle cramps in the body. Two teaspoonfuls of honey are taken at each meal, either directly from the spoon or combined with vinegar and water. If necessary, a tablespoonful of honey may also be taken at each meal to aid further in the control of pain.

These seven reasons, again, show why Vermont folk medicine prescribes honey for arthritis, as the result of trial and error for two centuries.

Furthermore, generations of Vermonters living close to the soil have made several other observations about honey and these have been passed along to succeeding generations:

1. Beekeepers do not have kidney trouble.
2. They have a clear complexion, good eyesight, and no lameness.
3. Among those who eat honey and keep bees there is no cancer or paralysis.

I spent two years checking that observation that beekeepers do not have cancer. Charles Mraz, of Middlebury, Vermont, the largest beekeeper in New England, helped me in this study. Together we were unable, in two years, to find a single case of cancer in beekeepers, or learn of one who had died of the disease. We did find a case of Hodgkin's disease, contracted before the man started keeping bees and eating honey. It was cured after he began his new occupation. Hodgkin's disease is a disorder of the body's glands, with a glandular enlargement that begins on one side of the neck and extends to other glands in the body.

Now let us consider why, in the treatment of arthritis, a drop of Lugol's solution of iodine is added to a glass of water containing two teaspoonfuls of apple cider vinegar and two of honey at one meal on Monday, Wednesday, and Friday of each week.

Reason One: Vermont folk medicine has learned that iodine is related to the ability to resist disease. Lugol's solution of iodine is prescribed in arthritis to enable the individual to avoid sickness that might make the arthritis worse by weakening the individual's power of resistance.

Reason Two: When I prescribed Lugol's solution for a patient I noted that he often later reported an improvement in his arthritis, if he had that ailment besides the one for which I was treating him. This was a side result that interested me very much.

Reason Three: Iodine is necessary for the thyroid gland's proper performance of its work. This gland is located in the front part of the neck. All the blood in the body passes through it every seventeen minutes. Because the cells making up the gland have an affinity for iodine its secretion of iodine during this seventeen-minute passage kills weak germs that may have gained entry into the blood through an injury to the skin, the lining of the nose or throat, or through the air breathed in, or the absorption of food from the digestive tract.

Strong, virulent germs are made weaker during their passage through the thyroid gland. With every seventeen-minute passage they are made still weaker until finally they are killed, if the gland has its normal supply of iodine. If it does not, it cannot kill these germs circulating in the blood, as nature intended it should.

It is well established that the iodine content of the thyroid gland is dependent on the iodine available in the individual's food and water intake. If the iodine intake is low the gland is deprived of an element it needs to do its work.

Reason Four: We learn from Vermont folk medicine, however, that the thyroid gland performs other functions besides killing harmful germs. It also rebuilds the energy with which we do our day's work, and so there is a definite relationship between the amount of energy you have and your iodine intake.

Reason Five: Another function of iodine is to calm the body and relieve nervous tension. When tension is high there is irritability and difficulty in sleeping. The body is constantly on a combat basis, organized for fight and flight. Therefore it badly needs iodine to lessen nervous tension and enable it to organize for peace and quiet, as well as to build and store body reserves against the time of need.

Reason Six: Still another function of iodine in the human body relates to clear thinking. The mind simply works better when it is supplied with the iodine it needs.

These are the reasons for taking iodine. A few words might be added on how to take it. Lugol's solution of iodine is an inexpensive preparation, and when it is used to maintain the body's iodine content the dose is small and needs to be taken only on certain days of the week. There is little of it to be found naturally in the body, no more than a trace.

It may be added to the vinegar-honey-and-water solution, one drop at one meal on Monday, Wednesday, and Friday every week. Hold the medicine dropped horizontally, so that you will get a larger drop. Stir the contents of the glass with a spoon and sip it during the meal.

Iodine is not the only extra weapon Vermont folk medicine prescribes to fight arthritis. In treating the disease the folk medicine way it is argued that the individual's body often needs to be rebuilt. It is like a piece of land that has worn out, and a general program of body building is needed in addition to the treatment directed specifically toward improving the arthritic condition. In rehabilitation one turns quite naturally to the kelp tablets marketed by Philip R.

Park, Inc., of San Pedro, California. There are two major reasons for using them.

First, Parkelp tablets are prescribed in arthritis as a food supplement because the composition of seven gallons of ocean water and that of the human body are the same, as I have pointed out before. Kelp grown in the ocean, therefore, has in it that which the human body needs. Ocean water represents our best soil. Kelp is grown in the ocean, in accordance with nature's plan, and there is no interference by man in its growth.

Second, the finished kelp product, according to reliable Norwegian sources, contains at least sixty minerals or elements, more than twelve vitamins, and twenty-one amino acids, all in balance. Kelp added to animal feed protects against deficiency diseases. The human body takes what it needs of these elements and has the ability to eliminate what it has no use for at the time, because it is equipped to handle minerals in organic form.

In taking Parkelp tablets for arthritis the patient begins by swallowing one at breakfast. It may be taken before, during, or after the meal, whichever is preferred. This dosage is continued at the same time every day for a week, and that may prove to be all that is necessary to bring about an improvement.

If you want to experiment, however, you may take at the beginning of the second week one tablet at the evening meal, in addition to the one taken at breakfast. At the beginning of the third week one tablet may be taken at each meal during the day. In Vermont patients do not accept more than three tablets a day. If I increase the dose beyond that a looseness of the bowels is likely to develop. In other parts of the country, I understand, more than three can be taken without this side effect.

I have observed in my Vermont practice at least five prime results from taking one Parkelp tablet at breakfast every day for a year in the treatment of arthritis:

1. There is less pain.
2. Swelling of joints does not increase.
3. The heart damaged by rheumatic fever earlier in life is much improved in its action.
4. Shortness of breath is no longer present.
5. The patient has much more energy.

Besides the aids I have been discussing in this chapter Vermont folk medicine prescribes certain local treatments in arthritis. This is done by making a solution of three cups of water and a half-cup of vinegar in a basin. Arthritic hands are soaked in this solution, when it is comfortably hot, for ten minutes, night and morning. As a result the swelling decreases, the joint action increases, and the grip returns to the hand so that objects may be grasped and held by the fingers.

If arthritis is present in the feet enough of the solution is made up to cover them. They are then soaked for ten minutes night and morning. For joints like the knee a cloth is wrung out of the solution and wrapped around, then a dry cloth is applied over the wet one to hold in the heat. As the cloth cools it is wrung out and applied again. The solution may be used repeatedly instead of making a new one every time as long as the odor of vinegar is quite noticeable.

The theory behind this treatment goes back to our observation of how a quart of water boiled in a teakettle enables deposited calcium to enter into solution. The natural conclusion is that if hands and feet are soaked in a hot solution of vinegar and water, calcium deposited in them will again enter into solution, with resulting improvement in the arthritis. The same thing would be true of the calcium in the joints when the solution is applied to them by means of a cloth.

In addition to this treatment the biologic food selection program I have described earlier should also be followed every day.

To conclude, let me summarize what Vermont folk medicine prescribes for the treatment of arthritis, based on the trial-and-error method developed over two centuries. The treatment has been considerably simplified with time, and today consists of the following five steps:

1. Two teaspoonfuls of apple cider vinegar and two of honey in a glass of water, taken at each meal. If, for any reason, this mixture is not accepted by the stomach at mealtimes it may be taken between meals—midmorning, midafternoon, or evening.
2. On Monday, Wednesday, and Friday of each week, at one meal on each of these days, a drop of Lugol's solution of iodine is added to the glass of water containing the vinegar-and-honey solution.

3. One Parkelp tablet is taken at breakfast or at all three meals, whichever gives the best results.

4. A solution made from a half-cup of vinegar and three cups of water is used to soak the hands and feet. It is applied by a cloth wrung out of this comfortably hot solution to other joints.

5. Biologic food selection is followed every day. This removes wheat foods, wheat cereals, white sugar, cirtrus fruits and their juices, and muscle meats like beef, lamb, and pork from the daily food intake. In the majority of individuals these foods produce an unwanted alkaline urine reaction when taken on rising in the morning.

Vermont folk medicine uses the same treatment for rheumatoid arthritis, osteoarthritis, gout, and bursitis. It does not differentiate between these but considers them as being manifestations of arthritis which are favorably influenced by the same treatment.

If one studies arthritis many years from the Vermont folk medicine viewpoint in time he comes to recognize it as an energy disease, due to a permanent organization of the energy expending mechanism of the body. All the folk medicine remedies used in the treatment of arthritis are those that end the permanent activity of the energy expending mechanism and bring peace and quiet to the body.

By favorably influencing the nervous, chemical, and endocrine parts of the energy expending mechanism the human motor is shifted from high to low gear. That is not only the essential approach to the treatment of arthritis, but the key to every man's good health.

Index